NATURE
— OF —
ALASKA

AN INTRODUCTION TO FAMILIAR PLANTS AND ANIMALS AND NATURAL ATTRACTIONS

WATERFORD PRESS

Reviews for the companion guide, *The Nature of California:*

"*The Nature of California* offers an agreeable overview of animals and plants casual hikers and campers are likely to encounter . . . a useful book to keep with the picnic supplies or camping gear."

LA Times

"With so many detailed guides in print, it would be tempting to overlook this book, yet it fills a valuable niche. Small and light, [it features] lovely color illustrations of several hundred species of plants, mammals, reptiles, fish and birds."

San Francisco Chronicle

"A useful and informative guide . . . this is a user-friendly book with an excellent introduction."

Books of the Southwest Review

"A colorful paperback field guide for people of all ages."

California Biodiversity News

THE
NATURE
— OF —
ALASKA

AN INTRODUCTION TO
FAMILIAR PLANTS AND ANIMALS
AND NATURAL ATTRACTIONS

Series Created and Edited by James Kavanagh

Illustrations by Raymond Leung

Introduction by James C. Rettie

WATERFORD PRESS

Distributed to the trade in North America by Falcon Press, P.O. Box 1716, Helena, MT 59624. Phone (800) 582-2665.

Publisher's Cataloguing in Publication Data
Kavanagh, James Daniel, 1960-
The Nature of Alaska. An Introduction to Familiar Plants and Animals and Natural Attractions. Includes bibliographical references and index.
1. Natural History – Alaska. 2. Animals – Identification – Alaska.
3. Plants – Identification – Alaska. 4. Tourism – Alaska.

Library of Congress Catalogue Card Number: 96-61162
ISBN: 0-9640225-5-9

The introductory essay, "BUT A WATCH IN THE NIGHT" by JAMES C. RETTIE is from FOREVER THE LAND by RUSSELL AND KATE LORD. Copyright © 1950 by Harper and Brothers, renewed copyright © 1978 by Russell and Kate Lord. Reprinted with permission of HarperCollins Publishers.

The publisher would like to acknowledge the following organizations and individuals who assisted in the research and development of this guide:

The Alaska Department of Fish & Game   Kenneth M. Maas
The United States Geological Survey   Linda Snyder
The Alaska Department of Tourism   Richard Mattson
The U.S. Fish & Wildlife Service   Raymond Leung
The Gastineau Fish Hatchery   Katherine Lesack
The Discovery Foundation   Jill Kavanagh

Consulting Naturalists: Greg Streveler, Panthea Redwood

The maps and text on pages 24-29 are adapted from the publication *Ecosystems of Alaska*, copyright © the United States Geological Survey and are reproduced with permission. Some species copy is adapted from the *Wildlife Notebook Series* copyright © the Alaska Department of Fish & Game and is reproduced with permission.

While every attempt has been made to ensure the accuracy of the information in this guide, it is important to note that experts often disagree with one another regarding the common name, size, appearance, habitat, distribution and taxonomy of species. The publisher welcomes all comments and suggestions.

Printed in Hong Kong

CONTENTS

To my father, Aidan

THE NATURE OF ALASKA is intended to provide novice naturalists with a pocket reference to the state's familiar and distinctive species of plants and animals and outstanding natural attractions.

This guide's primary purpose is to introduce the reader to common plants and animals and to highlight the diversity of species found in Alaska. Its secondary purpose is to show how all species in each ecosystem found here – from lush forests to the wet tundra – depend on each other, directly and indirectly, for survival.

The guide opens with a brief introduction to evolution in order to highlight the similarities and differences between some major groups of plants and animals and show when each appeared in geologic time. The brilliant introductory essay by James C. Rettie provides a simplified view of the evolution of life on earth, and the role that man – the animal – has played to date.

J.D.K.

BUT A WATCH IN THE NIGHT

BY JAMES C. RETTIE

James C. Rettie wrote the following essay while working for the National Forest Service in 1948. In a flash of brilliance, he converted the statistics from an existing government pamphlet on soil erosion into an analogy for the ages.

OUT BEYOND OUR SOLAR SYSTEM there is a planet called Copernicus. It came into existence some four or five billion years before the birth of our earth. In due course of time it became inhabited by a race of intelligent men.

About 750 million years ago the Copernicans had developed the motion picture machine to a point well in advance of the stage that we have reached. Most of the cameras that we now use in motion picture work are geared to take twenty-four pictures per second on a continuous strip of film. When such film is run through a projector, it throws a series of images on the screen and these change with a rapidity that gives the visual impression of normal movement. If a motion is too swift for the human eye to see it in detail, it can be captured and artificially slowed down by means of the slow-motion camera. This one is geared to take many more shots per second – ninety-six or even more than that. When the slow motion film is projected at the normal speed of twenty-four pictures per second, we can see just how the jumping horse goes over a hurdle.

What about motion that is too slow to be seen by the human eye? That problem has been solved by the use of the time-lapse camera. In this one, the shutter is geared to take only one shot per second, or one per minute, or even one per hour – depending upon the kind of movement that is being photographed. When the time-lapse film is projected at the normal speed of twenty-four pictures per second, it is possible to see a bean sprout growing up out of the ground. Time-lapse films are useful in the study of many types of motion too slow to be observed by the unaided, human eye.

The Copernicans, it seems, had time-lapse cameras some 757 million years ago and they also had superpowered telescopes that gave them a clear view of what was happening upon this earth. They decided to make a film record of the life history of earth and to make it on the scale of one picture per year. The photography has been in progress during the last 757 million years.

In the near future, a Copernican interstellar expedition will arrive upon our earth and bring with it a copy of the time-lapse film. Arrangements will be made for showing the entire film in one continuous run. This will begin at midnight of New Year's eve and continue day and night without a single stop until midnight on December 31. The rate of projection will be 24 pictures per second. Time on the screen will thus seem to move at the rate of twenty-four years per second; 1440 years per minute; 86,400 years per hour; approximately two million years per day and sixty-two million years per month. The normal lifespan of individual man will occupy about three seconds. The full period of earth history that will be unfolded on the screen (some 757 million years) will extend from what the geologists call the Pre-Cambrian times up to the present. This will, by no means, cover the full time-span of the earth's geological history but it will embrace the period since the advent of living organisms.

During the months of January, February, and March the picture will be desolate and dreary. The shape of the land masses and the oceans will bear little or no resemblance to those that we know. The violence of geological erosion will be much in evidence. Rains will pour down on the land and promptly go booming down to the seas. There will be no clear streams anywhere except where the rains fall upon hard rock. Everywhere on the steeper ground the stream channels will be filled with boulders hurled down by rushing waters. Raging torrents and dry stream beds will keep alternating in quick succession. High mountains will seem to melt like so much butter in the sun. The shifting of land into the seas, later to be thrust up as new mountains, will be going on at a grand scale.

Early in April there will be some indication of the presence of single-celled living organisms in some of the warmer and sheltered coastal waters. By the end of the month it will be noticed that some of these organisms have become multicellular. A few of them, including the Trilobites, will be encased in hard shells.

Toward the end of May, the first vertebrates will appear, but they will still be aquatic creatures. In June about 60 per cent of the land area that we know as North America will be under water. One broad channel will occupy the space where the Rocky Mountains now stand. Great deposits of limestone will be forming under some of the shallower seas. Oil and gas deposits will be in process of formation – also under shallow seas. On land there will be no sign of vegetation. Erosion will be rampant, tearing loose particles and chunks of rock and grinding them into sand and silt to be spewed out by the streams into bays and estuaries.

About the middle of July the first land plants will appear and take up the tremendous job of soil building. Slowly, very slowly, the mat of vegetation will spread, always battling for its life against the power of erosion. Almost foot by foot, the plant life will advance, lacing down with its root structures whatever pulverized rock material it can find. Leaves and stems will be giving added protection against the loss of the soil foothold. The increasing vegetation will pave the way for the land animals that will live upon it.

Early in August the seas will be teeming with fish. This will be what geologists call the Devonian period. Some of the races of these fish will be breathing by means of lung tissue instead of through gill tissues. Before the month is over, some of the lung fish will go ashore and take on a crude lizard-like appearance. Here are the first amphibians.

In early September the insects will put in their appearance. Some will look like huge dragonflies and will have a wing span of 24 inches. Large portions of the land masses will now be covered with heavy vegetation that will include the primitive spore-propagating trees. Layer upon layer of this plant growth will build up, later to appear as coal deposits. About the middle of this month, there will be evidence of the first seed-bearing plants and the first reptiles. Heretofore, the land animals will have been amphibians that could reproduce their kind only by depositing a soft egg mass in quiet waters. The reptiles will be shown to be freed from the aquatic bond because they can reproduce by means of a shelled egg in which the embryo and its nurturing liquids are sealed and thus protected from destructive evaporation. Before September is over, the first dinosaurs will be seen – creatures destined to dominate the animal realm for about 140 million years and then to disappear.

In October there will be series of mountain uplifts along what is now the eastern coast of the United States. A creature with feathered limbs - half bird and half reptile in appearance – will take itself into the air. Some small and rather unpretentious animals will be seen to bring forth their young in a form that is a miniature replica of the parents and to feed these young on milk secreted by mammary glands in the female parent. The emergence of this mammalian form of animal life will be recognized as one of the great events in geologic time. October will also witness the high-water mark of the dinosaurs – creatures ranging in size from that of the modern goat to monsters like Brontosaurus that weighed some 40 tons. Most of them will be placid vegetarians, but a few will be hideous-looking carnivores, like Allosaurus and Tyrannosaurus. Some of the herbivorous dinosaurs will be clad in bony armor for protection against their flesh-eating comrades.

November will bring pictures of a sea extending from the Gulf of Mexico to the Arctic in space now occupied by the Rocky Mountains. A few of the reptiles will take to the air on bat-like wings. One of these, called Pteranodon, will have a wingspread of 15 feet. There will be a rapid development of the modern flowering plants, modern trees, and modern insects. The dinosaurs will disappear. Toward the end of the month there will be a tremendous land disturbance in which the Rocky Mountains will rise out of the sea to assume a dominating place in the North American landscape.

As the picture runs on into December it will show the mammals in command of the animal life. Seed-bearing trees and grasses will have covered most of the land with a heavy mantle of vegetation.

Only the areas newly thrust up from the sea will be barren. Most of the streams will be crystal clear. The turmoil of geological erosion will be confined to localized areas. About December 25 will begin the cutting of the Grand Canyon of the Colorado River. Grinding down through layer after layer of sedimentary strata, this stream will finally expose deposits laid down in Pre-Cambrian times. Thus in the walls of that canyon will appear geological formations dating from recent times to the period when the earth had no living organisms upon it.

The picture will run on through the latter days of December and even up to its final day with still no sign of mankind. The spectators will become alarmed in the fear that man has somehow been left out. But not so; sometime about noon on December 31 (one million years ago) will appear a stooped, massive creature of man-like proportions. This will be Pithecanthropus, the Java ape man. For tools and weapons he will have nothing but crude stone and wooden clubs. His children will live a precarious existence threatened on the one side by hostile animals and on the other by tremendous climatic changes. Ice sheets – in places 4,000 feet deep – will form in the northern parts of North America and Eurasia. Four times this glacial ice will push southward to cover half the continents. With each advance the plant and animal life will be swept under or pushed southward. With each recession of the ice, life will struggle to reestablish itself in the wake of the retreating glaciers. The woolly mammoth, the musk ox, and the caribou all will fight to maintain themselves near the ice line. Sometimes they will be caught and put into cold storage – skin, flesh, blood, bones, and all.

The picture will run on through supper time with still very little evidence of man's presence on earth. It will be about 11 o'clock when Neanderthal man appears. Another half hour will go by before the appearance of Cro-Magnon man living in caves and painting crude animal pictures on the walls of his dwelling. Fifteen minutes more will bring Neolithic man, knowing how to chip stone and thus produce sharp cutting edges for spears and tools. In a few minutes more it will appear that man has domesticated the dog, the sheep and, possibly, other animals. He will then begin the use of milk. He will also learn the arts of basket weaving and the making of pottery and dugout canoes.

The dawn of civilization will not come until about five or six minutes before the end of the picture. The story of the Egyptians, the Babylonians, the Greeks, and the Romans will unroll during the fourth, the third, and the second minute before the end. At 58 minutes and 43 seconds past 11:00 P.M. (just 1 minute and 17 seconds before the end) will come the beginning of the Christian era. Columbus will discover the new world 20 seconds before the end. The Declaration of Independence will be signed just 7 seconds before the final curtain comes down.

In those few moments of geologic time will be the story of all that has happened since we became a nation. And what a story it will be! A human swarm will sweep across the face of the continent and take it away from the [Native Americans]. They will change it far more radically than it has ever been changed before in a comparable time. The great virgin forests will be seen going down before ax and fire. The soil, covered for eons by its protective mantle of trees and grasses, will be laid bare to the ravages of water and wind erosion. Streams that had been flowing clear will, once again, take up a load of silt and push it toward the seas. Humus and mineral salts, both vital elements of productive soil, will be seen to vanish at a terrifying rate.

The railroads and highways and cities that will spring up may divert attention, but they cannot cover up the blight of man's recent activities. In great sections of Asia, it will be seen that man must utilize cow dung and every scrap of available straw or grass for fuel to cook his food. The forests that once provided wood for this purpose will be gone without a trace. The use of these agricultural wastes for fuel, in place of returning them to the land, will be leading to increasing soil impoverishment. Here and there will be seen a dust storm darkening the landscape over an area a thousand miles across. Man-creatures will be shown counting their wealth in terms of bits of printed paper representing other bits of a scarce but comparatively useless yellow metal that is kept buried in strong vaults. Meanwhile, the soil, the only real wealth that can keep mankind alive on the face of this earth is savagely being cut loose from its ancient moorings and washed into the seven seas.

We have just arrived upon this earth. How long will we stay?

This guide describes more than 275 species of plants and animals that are common in Alaska. The term 'common' is intended to refer to those species which are abundant, widely distributed and easy to observe in the field. A few less common and more localized species have also been included to provide readers with insight into the diversity of organisms found in Alaska.

Throughout the book, plants and animals are arranged more-or-less in their taxonomic groupings. Exceptions have been made when non-traditional groupings facilitate field identification for the novice (e.g., wildflowers are grouped by color).

Because this guide has been written for the novice, every attempt has been made to simplify presentation of the material. Illustrations are accompanied by brief descriptions of key features, and technical terms have been held to a minimum throughout.

SPECIES TEXT

The species descriptions have been fragmented to simplify presentation of information:

GROUND CONE
The name in bold type indicates the common name of the species. It is important to note that a single species may have many common names. The above plant is also commonly called 'broomrape.'

Boschniakia rossica
The italicized latin words refer to an organism's scientific name, a universally accepted two-part term that precisely defines its relationship to other organisms. The first capitalized word, the genus, refers to groups of closely related organisms. The second term, the species name, refers to organisms that look similar and interbreed freely. If the second word in the term is '*spp.*', this indicates there are several species in the genus that look similar to the one illustrated. If a third word appears in the term, it identifies a subspecies, a group of individuals that are even more closely related.

Size
Generally indicates the average length of animals (nose to tail tip) and the average height of plants. Exceptions are noted in the text.

Description
Refers to key markings and/or characteristics that help to distinguish a species.

Habitat
>Where a species lives/can be found.

Comments
>General information regarding distinctive behaviors, diet, vocalizations, related species, etc.

ILLUSTRATIONS

The majority of animal illustrations show the adult male in its breeding coloration. Plant illustrations are designed to highlight the characteristics that are most conspicuous in the field. It is important to note that illustrations are merely meant as guidelines; coloration, size and shape will vary depending on age, sex or season.

CHECKLISTS

The checklists at the back of this book are provided to allow you to keep track of the plants and animals you identify.

TIPS ON FIELD IDENTIFICATION

Identifying a species in the field can be as simple as one-two-three:

>1. Note key markings, characteristics and/or behaviors;
>2. Find an illustration that matches; and
>3. Read the text to confirm your sighting.

Identifying mammals or birds in the field is not fundamentally different than identifying trees, flowers or other forms of life. It is simply a matter of knowing what to look for. Reading the introductory text to each section will make you aware of key characteristics of each group and allow you to use the guide more effectively in the field.

N.B. – We refer primarily to common species in this guide and do not list all species within any group. References listed in the bibliography at the back of this guide provide more detailed information about specific areas of study.

EVOLUTION OF ANIMALS

WHAT IS AN ANIMAL?

Animals are living organisms which can generally be distinguished from plants in four ways:
1) they feed on plants and other animals;
2) they have a nervous system;
3) they can move freely and are not rooted; and
4) their cells do not have rigid walls or contain chlorophyll.

All animals are members of the animal kingdom, a group consisting of more than a million species. Species are classified within the animal kingdom according to their evolutionary relationships to one another.

Most of the animals discussed in this guide are members of the group called vertebrates. They all possess backbones and most have complex brains and highly developed senses.

The earliest vertebrates appeared in the oceans about 500 million years ago. Today, surviving species are divided into five main groups.

- Fishes
- Amphibians
- Reptiles
- Birds
- Mammals

Following is a simplified description of the evolution of the vertebrates and the differences between groups.

FISHES

The oldest form of vertebrate life, fishes evolved from invertebrate sea creatures 400-500 million years ago. All are cold-blooded (ectothermic) and their activity levels are largely influenced by the surrounding environment.

The first species were armored and jawless and fed by filtering tiny organisms from water and mud. Surviving members of this group include lampreys and hagfishes. Jawless fishes were succeeded by jawed fishes that quickly came to dominate the seas, and still do today. The major surviving groups include:

1) Sharks and rays – more primitive species which possess soft skeletons made of cartilage; and
2) Bony fishes – a more advanced group of fishes that have bony skeletons, it includes most of the fishes found today.

Physiological Characteristics of Fishes

Heart and gills

A two-chambered heart circulates the blood through a simple system of arteries and veins. Gills act like lungs and allow fish to absorb dissolved oxygen from the water into their bloodstream.

Nervous system

Small anterior brain is connected to a spinal cord which runs the length of the body.

Digestive system

Digestive system is complete. A number of specialized organs produce enzymes which help to break down food in the stomach and intestines. Kidneys extract urine from the blood and waste is eliminated through the anus.

Reproduction

In most fishes, the female lays numerous eggs in water and the male fertilizes them externally. Young usually hatch as larvae, and the larval period ranges from a few hours to several years. Survival rate of young is low.

Senses

Most have the senses of taste, touch, smell, hearing and sight, though their vision is generally poor. Fishes hear and feel by sensing vibrations and temperature and pressure changes in the surrounding water.

AMPHIBIANS

The first limbed land-dwellers, amphibians evolved from fishes 300-400 million years ago and became the dominant land vertebrates for more than 100 million years. Like fishes, amphibians are cold-blooded and their activity levels are largely influenced by the environment.

Some believe that the first amphibians arose because of the intense competition for survival in the water. The first fish-like amphibian ancestors to escape the water were those that had the ability to breathe air and possessed strong, paired fins that allowed them to wriggle onto mud-flats and sandbars. (Living relics of this group include five species of lungfish and the rare coelacanth.) Though amphibians were able to exploit rich new habitats on land, they remained largely dependent on aquatic environments for survival and reproduction.

The major surviving groups are:

1) Salamanders – slender-bodied, short-legged, long-tailed creatures that live secretive lives in dark, damp areas; and
2) Frogs and toads – squat-bodied, animals with long hind legs, large heads and large eyes, they are common residents of rural and urban ponds and lakes.

Advances Made Over Fishes

Lungs and legs

By developing lungs and legs, amphibians freed themselves from the competition for food in aquatic environments and were able to flourish on land.

Improved circulatory system

Amphibians evolved a heart with three chambers that enhanced gas exchange in the lungs and provided body tissues with highly oxygenated blood.

Ears

Frogs and toads developed external ears that enhanced their hearing ability, an essential adaptation for surviving on land.

Reproduction

Most amphibians reproduce like fish. Salamanders differ in that most fertilize eggs internally rather than externally. In many, the male produces a sperm packet which the female collects and uses to fertilize eggs as they are laid.

REPTILES

Reptiles appeared 300-350 million years ago. They soon came to dominate the earth, and continued to rule the land, sea and air for more than 130 million years. Cold-blooded like amphibians, reptiles evolved a host of characteristics that made them better suited for life on land.

About 65 million years ago, the dominant reptiles mysteriously underwent a mass extinction. A popular theory suggests this was caused by a giant meteor hitting the earth which sent up a huge dust cloud that blotted out the sun. The lack of sun and subsequently low temperatures caused many plants and animals to perish.

The major surviving reptilian groups are:

1) Turtles – hard-shelled reptiles with short legs;
2) Lizards – scaly-skinned reptiles with long legs and tails;
3) Snakes – long, legless reptiles with scaly skin; and
4) Crocodilians – very large reptiles with elongate snouts, toothy jaws and long tails.

Advances Made Over Amphibians

Reproduction

Fertilization is by copulation and females lay leathery, shelled eggs. The development of the shelled egg was the single most important evolutionary advancement for the group since this freed them from dependence on a watery environment and allowed them to exploit new habitats on land unchallenged. The young do not go through a larval stage and are independent from birth.

Dry, scaly skin
> Their dry skin prevents water loss and also protects them from predators.

Posture
> Many reptiles evolved an upright posture and strong legs which enhanced their mobility on land.

Improved heart and lungs
> Their heart and lungs are more efficient and heightened their activity levels. The heart had four chambers (although the division between ventricles was usually incomplete), and it was therefore less likely that oxygenated and deoxygenated blood would mix.

Defense
> They are agile and better able to defend themselves, having sharp claws and teeth or beaks capable of inflicting wounds.

BIRDS

Birds evolved from reptiles 100-200 million years ago. Unlike species before them, birds were warm-blooded (endothermic) and able to regulate their body temperature internally.* This meant that they could maintain high activity levels despite fluctuations in environmental temperature. They are believed to have evolved from a group of gliding reptiles, with their scaly legs considered proof of their reptilian heritage.

*There is still a debate over whether or not some dinosaurs were warm-blooded.

Advances Made Over Reptiles
Ability to fly
> By evolving flight, birds were able to exploit environments that were inaccessible to their competitors and predators. The characteristics they evolved that allowed them to fly included wings, feathers, hollow bones, an enhanced breathing capacity.

Warm-blooded
> An insulating layer of feathers enhances their capacity to retain heat. They also have true four-chambered hearts.

Keen senses
> Birds evolved very keen senses of vision and hearing and developed complex behavioral and communicative patterns.

Reproduction
> Fertilization is internal and the eggs have hard, rather than leathery, shells. Unlike most reptiles, birds incubate their eggs themselves and protect and nurture their young for a period of time following birth.

MAMMALS

Mammals evolved from reptiles 100-200 million years ago. Though warm-blooded like birds, they are believed to have different reptilian ancestors. In addition to being warm-blooded, mammals also evolved physiological adaptations which allowed them to hunt prey and avoid predation better than their competititors.

Mammals quickly exploited the habitats left vacant by the dinosaurs and have been the dominant land vertebrates for the past 65 million years. Man is a relatively new addition to the group, having a lineage of less than three million years.

Mammals have evolved into three distinct groups, all of which have living representatives:

1) <u>Monotremes</u> – egg-laying mammals (the platypus and echidna);
2) <u>Marsupials</u> – pouched mammals which bear living, embryonic young; and
3) <u>Placentals</u> – mammals which bear fully-developed young.

Advances Made Over Birds

<u>Reproduction</u>

Fertilization is internal but in most the young develop in the female's uterus instead of an egg. After birth, the young are fed and nurtured by adults for an extensive period, during which they learn behavioral lessons from their elders and siblings. This emphasis on learned responses at an early age is believed to contribute to the superior intelligence and reproductive success of the group.

<u>Hearing</u>

Most have three bones in the middle ear to enhance hearing. (Birds and reptiles have one.)

<u>Teeth</u>

Many developed specialized teeth that allowed them to rely on a variety of food sources. Incisors were for cutting, canines for tearing and molars for chewing or shearing.

<u>Breathing</u>

Mammals evolved a diaphragm which increases breathing efficiency.

<u>Posture</u>

Many have long, strong legs and are very agile on land.

EVOLUTION OF PLANTS

WHAT IS A PLANT?

Plants are living organisms which can generally be distinguished from animals in four ways:

1) they synthesize their own food needed for maintenance and growth from carbon dioxide, water and sunlight;
2) they do not have a nervous system;
3) most are rooted and cannot move around easily; and
4) their cells have rigid walls and contain chlorophyll, a pigment needed for photosynthesis.

All plants are members of the plant kingdom. According to the fossil record, plants evolved from algae that originated nearly three billion years ago. Since then, plants have evolved into millions of species in a mind-boggling assortment of groups.

Since plant classification is complex, we will limit our discussion to two groups which encompass many of the most familiar plants, namely:

1) Gymnosperms – plants with naked seeds;
2) Angiosperms – flowering plants with enclosed seeds.

GYMNOSPERMS – THE NAKED SEED PLANTS

This group of mostly evergreen trees and shrubs includes some of the largest and oldest known plants. They began to appear around 300-400 million years ago, and were the dominant plant species on earth for nearly 200 million years. The most successful surviving group of gymnosperms are the conifers, which include such species as pines, spruces, firs, larches and junipers.

Most conifers are evergreen and have small needle-like or scale-like leaves which are adapted to withstand extreme temperature changes. Some species are deciduous, but most retain their leaves for two or more years before shedding them.

Reproduction

Most evergreens produce woody 'cones'– conical fruits that contain the male and female gametes. The male cones produce pollen that is carried by the wind to settle between the scales of female cones on other trees. The pollen stimulates ovules to change into seeds, and the scales of the female cone close up to protect the seeds. When the seeds are ripe – up to two years later – environmental conditions stimulate the cone to open its scales and the naked seeds fall to the ground.

ANGIOSPERMS – THE FLOWERING PLANTS

Angiosperms first appeared in the fossil record around 130 million years ago. They quickly adapted to a wide variety of environments and succeeded gymnosperms as the dominant land plants. Their reproductive success was largely due to two key adaptations:

1) They produced flowers which attracted pollinating agents such as insects and birds; and
2) They produced seeds encased in 'fruits', to aid in seed dispersal.

Angiosperms make up a diverse and widespread group of plants ranging from trees and shrubs such as oaks, cherries, maples, hazelnuts, and apples, to typical flowers like lilies, orchids, roses, daisies, and violets. The trees and shrubs within this group are commonly referred to as 'deciduous', and most shed their leaves annually.

Reproduction

A typical flower has colorful petals that encircle the male and female reproductive structures (see illustration in introduction to wildflowers). The male stamens are composed of thin filaments supporting anthers containing pollen. The female pistil contains unfertilized seeds in the swollen basal part called the ovary. Pollination occurs when pollen — carried by the wind or animals — reaches the pistil.

Once fertilization has occurred, the ovules develop into seeds and the ovary into a fruit. The fruit and seeds mature together, with the fruit ripening to the point where the seeds are capable of germinating. At maturity, each seed contains an embryo and a food supply to nourish it upon germination. Upon ripening, the fruit may fall to the ground with the seeds still inside, as in peaches, cherries, and squash, or it may burst open and scatter its seeds in the wind, like poplar trees, willows, and dandelions.

Fruit comes in many forms, from grapes, tomatoes, apples, and pears, to pea and bean pods, nuts, burrs and capsules. Regardless of its shape, fruit enhances the reproductive success of angiosperms in two important ways. First, it helps to protect the seeds from the elements until they have fully matured, enabling them to survive unfavorable conditions. Secondly, fruit aids in seed dispersal. Some fruits are eaten by animals that eventually release the seeds in their feces, an ideal growing medium. Others may be spiny or burred so they catch on the coats of animals, or may have special features which enable them to be carried away from their parent plant by the wind or water.

GEOLOGICAL TIMESCALE

ERA	PERIOD	MYA*	EVENTS
CENOZOIC	HOLOCENE	.01	Dominance of man.
	QUATERNARY	2.5	First human civilizations.
	TERTIARY	65	Mammals, birds, insects and angiosperms dominate the land.
MESOZOIC	CRETACEOUS	135	Dinosaurs extinct. Mammals, insects and angiosperms undergo great expansion. Gymnosperms decline.
	JURASSIC	190	Age of Reptiles; dinosaurs dominant. First birds appear.
	TRIASSIC	225	First dinosaurs and mammals appear. Gymnosperms are dominant plants.
PALEOZOIC	PERMIAN	280	Great expansion of reptiles causes amphibians to decline. Many marine invertebrates become extinct.
	CARBONIFEROUS	340	Age of Amphibians; amphibians dominant. First reptiles appear. Fish undergo a great expansion.
	DEVONIAN	400	Age of Fishes; fishes dominant. First amphibians, insects and gymnosperms appear.
	SILURIAN	430	First jawed fishes appear. Plants move onto land.
	ORDOVICIAN	500	First vertebrates appear.
	CAMBRIAN	600	Marine invertebrates and algae abundant.

*Millions of years ago

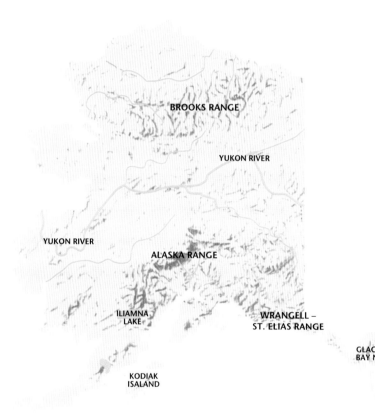

BROOKS RANGE

YUKON RIVER

YUKON RIVER

ALASKA RANGE

ILIAMNA
LAKE

WRANGELL –
ST. ELIAS RANGE

GLACIER
BAY N.P.

KODIAK
ISALAND

ALEUTIAN ISLANDS

Geography

Highest Point: 20,320 ft. (6,193 m) Mount McKinley
Area: 586,000 sq. mi. (938,000 sq. km)

Outstanding Features

Mountain Ranges

Alaska's 39 mountain ranges include 17 of the 20 highest mountains found in the U.S. The highest point in North America, Mount McKinley, is the located in the heart of the Alaska Range. Other dominant ranges include the northern Brooks Range, part of which is contained within the renowned Arctic National Wildlife Refuge. The southeastern Wrangell-St. Elias Range contains 9 of the highest peaks in the U.S.

Rivers

Over 25 of Alaska's 3,000 rivers have been designated National Wild and Scenic Rivers because of their exceptional natural features. Floating the rivers is a popular mode of travel to the state's remote areas during summer months. The mighty Yukon River, the fourth longest river in North America, stretches for 1,400 miles (2,253 km) through central Alaska.

Lakes

It is estimated that Alaska has more than three million lakes. They vary in size from shallow tundra ponds to the 1,000 square-mile (1,609 sq. km) Iliamna Lake west of Anchorage. The majority are located along the north and west coasts in the wet tundra system at or near sea level. A total of 107 major lakes – those with a surface area of over 10 square miles (16 sq. km) and/or depths in excess of 250 ft. (76 m) – have been identified.

Glaciers

Over 5% of Alaska is covered by these massive moving ice fields that continually sculpt the surrounding landscape. Glaciers originate in mountainous areas where snows accumulate over many years. Over time, the weight of the snow compresses the lower layers into ice. As glaciers warm and cool, they push against mountainsides and slowly grate and grind rock in the process. A number of southern glaciers terminate in the ocean where chunks break off ('calve') forming icebergs. Glacier Bay National Park encompasses 20 tidewater glaciers.

Islands

Alaska has thousands of islands, 1,800 of which have been named. The largest Island in the state, Kodiak Island, covers 3,588 sq. mi. (5,744 sq. km). The volcanic Aleutian Island chain in the southwest contains more than 200 individual islands.

ECOSYSTEMS

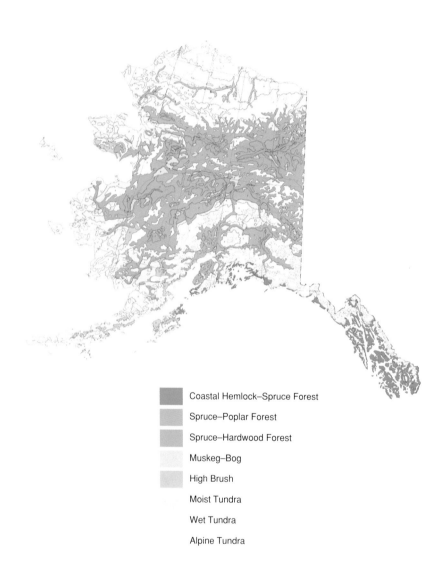

Coastal Hemlock–Spruce Forest

Spruce–Poplar Forest

Spruce–Hardwood Forest

Muskeg–Bog

High Brush

Moist Tundra

Wet Tundra

Alpine Tundra

Ecosystems

Coastal Hemlock–Spruce Forest

This dense evergreen forest ecosystem is comprised primarily of western hemlock and Sitka spruce, with a scattering of mountain hemlock, lodgepole pine, and, in the extreme southeast, western red cedar and Alaska cedar. Black cottonwood and alder are common along streams, rivers, beach fringes and recent clearcuts. Throughout much of the system the forest understory has blueberry, devilsclub, skunk cabbage and ferns amid a carpet of moss. Low shrubs, sedges, grasses, and mosses are common in poorly-drained lowland areas.

This ecosystem is found on steep mountain slopes and valleys bordering the Pacific coast as well as other areas.

Spruce–Poplar Forest

This tall, relatively dense interior forest system is composed primarily of white spruce and balsam poplar. The undergrowth is generally dense, consisting of high and low shrubs including alder, willow, rose, dogwood, Labrador tea and berries. The forest floor is usually carpeted with ferns, fireweed, horsetails, herbs and moss.

Spruce-poplar forests are typically confined to broad floodplains and river terraces in central Alaska to elevations up to 1,000 ft. (305 m).

Spruce–Hardwood Forest

This forest system is dominated by white spruce, black spruce, birch, aspen and poplar. Black spruce typically grows on north slopes and poorly drained flat areas. The slow-growing stunted tamarack is associated with black spruce north of the Alaska Range. White spruce occur in mixed stands on south facing slopes and well drained soils, forming pure stands near streams. Rolling lowlands have a varied mixture of white spruce, black spruce, paper birch, aspen and poplar. Small bogs and muskegs are found in the depressions. Typical plants include willow, alder, ferns, rose, high and low bush cranberry, raspberry, dwarf birch, blueberry, Labrador tea, crowberry, bearberry, cottongrass and horsetail.

Muskeg-Bog

Muskeg-bogs are usually found in areas where drainage is poor and conditions are too wet for tree growth. This system is found in two areas: Coastal muskeg-bogs are found in depressions, flat areas, and gentle slopes where drainage is poor and commonly consist of a thick sphagnum moss mat, sedges, rushes,lichens, cottongrass, Labrador tea, common juniper, crowberry, willow, bog cranberry, and bog blueberry. A few slow-growing, poorly formed shore pine, western hemlock or Alaska cedar are scattered on drier sites. Shrubs are dominant in exposed and drier areas. Interior muskeg-bogs occur on old river terraces, filling ponds, and old sloughs and consist of varying amounts of sedges, mosses, bog rosemary, dwarf birch, Labrador tea, willow, cranberry, and blueberry. Localized saturated flats have large patches of cotton grass. South of the Alaska Range, these bogs occur in former glacial lake basins and flat areas of the lower Yukon and Kuskokwim Rivers.

High Brush

These are dense to open deciduous brush systems. Floodplain thickets occur along interior rivers and are dominated by willow and alder shrubs and associated species including dogwood, prickly rose, raspberry and high bush cranberry. Birch-alder-willow thickets are found near timberlines in interior Alaska and consist of birch, green alder and several willow species. Other associated species are Sitka alder, bearberry, crowberry, Labrador tea, spirea, blueberry, and cranberry. Coastal alder thickets which fringe the forest along beaches, streams and alpine and avalanche areas are dominated by Sitka alder and associated species including devilsclub, willow, currant, thimbleberry, salmonberry, blueberry and huckleberry.

Moist Tundra

Moist tundra ecosystems usually form a complete ground cover and some are extremely productive during the growing season. They vary from almost continuous and uniformly developed cottongrass tussocks to stands where tussocks are scarce or lacking and dwarf shrubs are dominant. Associated species are mosses, alpine azalea, mountain-avens, low-growing willows, dwarf birch, Labrador tea, green alder, Lapland rosebay, bog blueberry and mountain cranberry.

Moist tundra occurs along beaches and rolling foothills in north Alaska, on volcanic hills in the Yukon delta, on lower mountain slopes in the Aleutian Islands, on high foothills along the Alaska Range and the Copper River basin and elsewhere, including the Anchorage area.

Wet Tundra

This system is usually found in flat areas with shallow lakes. Dominant vegetation is sedge and cottongrass. A few woody and herbaceous plants occur on the drier sites above the water table. Rooted aquatic plants occur along shorelines and in shallower lakes. Associated plants are mosses, low-growing willows, dwarf birch, Labrador tea, cinquefoil, low bush cranberry and occasionally bog cranberry. Characteristic rooted aquatic plants are bur-reed, pondweed and mare's tail.

Wet tundra is extensive along the coastal plains north of the Brooks Range, the northern part of the Seward Peninsula, Selawik Basin, Yukon-Kuskokwim Delta and Bristol Bay Lowland, Aleutian Islands, Alaska Peninsula, and the Copper River Delta.

Alpine Tundra

Alpine tundra systems are found on all mountain ranges of Alaska, and on exposed ridges in the Arctic and southwestern coastal areas. The system consists of barren rocks and rubble interspersed with low plant mats. White mountain-avens are dominant in northern areas and in the Alaska Range. They may cover entire ridges and slopes along with low growing herbs such as moss campion, lichens, grasses and sedges.

In southeastern coastal mountains and the Aleutian Islands the most prominent plants are low heath shrubs, especially cassiopes and mountain-heaths. They are most abundant where accumulated snow lingers into late spring. On the Aleutian Islands, this system consists primarily of crowberry, bog blueberry, mountain cranberry, alpine azalea and dwarf willows. Associated species are dwarf birch, cassiope, crowberry, Labrador tea, mountain heath, dwarf blueberry, bog blueberry and cranberry.

Alpine tundra occurs on rocky ridges and mountain tops above 2,500 feet elevations (762 m) in the Brooks Range, above 4,000 feet (1,219 m) in the Alaska Range, above 1,000 feet (305 m) in the Aleutian Islands and above treeline in central and southeast Alaska.

CLIMATE ZONES

ARCTIC

CONTINENTAL

TRANSITIONAL

MARITIME

Climate

The National Weather Service recognizes four major climatic zones in Alaska: Arctic; Continental; Transitional; and Maritime. These zones are briefly described in the table below:

Climatic Zone	Annual Precipitation (inches)			Annual Temperature (F°)		
	Max.	Min.	Avg.	Max.	Min.	Avg.
ARCTIC	21	4	7	90	-61	10-20
CONTINENTAL	24	10	15	100	-75	15-25
TRANSITIONAL	30	12	17	90	-70	22-35
MARITIME	300	11	65	99	-42	33-45

The recorded annual precipitation ranges from 4 in. (10 cm) in the Arctic to 300 in. (7.6 m) along the southeast coast. The mean annual temperatures for the State vary from 10° to 45°F (-12 to 7°C). The temperature extremes vary from a high of 100°F (37.7°C) to a low of -75°F (-59.4°C).

Near the Arctic Circle (66°30 N), the sun remains above the horizon on June 21 and 22. At Barrow, it remains above the horizon continuously for 85 days. Correspondingly, in midwinter, it remains below the horizon for 67 days.

The annual activity and distribution of Alaska's plants and animals is greatly affected by the climate. Animals have adapted to cold through migration, insulation, hibernation or other modes of energy conservation. Annual plants are shallow-rooted and capable of producing mature seeds in short summers. Perennials have cells with walls resilient enough to avoid rupturing when frozen. Most plants are hardy, with tough stems, branches and roots capable of withstanding extreme conditions.

WHAT ARE MAMMALS?

Most mammals are warm-blooded, furred creatures that have four feet and a tail and several different kinds of teeth. All North American species give birth to live young which feed on milk from their mother's mammary glands.

HOW TO IDENTIFY MAMMALS

Mammals are generally secretive in their habits and therefore difficult to spot in the field. The best time to look for mammals is usually at dusk/dawn and at night when they are often foraging.

When you spot a mammal, note its size, shape, and color. Check for distinguishing field marks and consider the surrounding habitat.

COMMON TRACKS

Studying tracks is one way to discover the kinds of mammals found in your area. For more information on animal tracks, see the references under mammals in the bibliography of this guide.

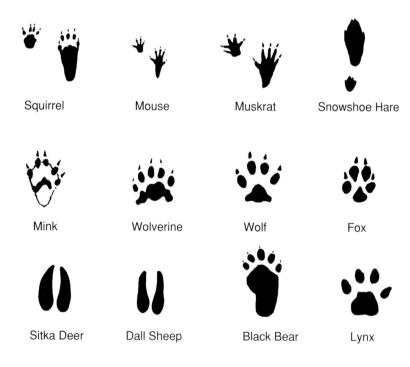

Squirrel	Mouse	Muskrat	Snowshoe Hare
Mink	Wolverine	Wolf	Fox
Sitka Deer	Dall Sheep	Black Bear	Lynx

N.B. – *Tracks are not to scale*

INSECTIVORES

Insectivores are generally small mammals with long snouts, short legs and sharp teeth. They live on or under the ground and feed on insects and other invertebrates. Shrews are Alaska's smallest mammals.

MASKED SHREW
Sorex cinereus
Size: 3-4 in. (7-10 cm)
Description: Gray-brown, mouse-like mammal with a long, pointed nose and a long tail.
Habitat: Moist habitats throughout most of Alaska.
Comments: Active throughout the year, it is one of nine species of shrew found in Alaska. Like all shrews, it has a very high metabolic rate and must eat voraciously to stay alive. Characterized as nervous and aggressive, shrews will kill each other if confined in an enclosed area.

BATS

The only true flying mammals, bats have large ears, small eyes and broad wings. Primarily nocturnal, they have developed a sophisticated sonar system – echolocation – to help them hunt insects at night. As they fly, they emit a series of high frequency sounds that bounce off objects and tell them what lies in their path. During daylight, they seek refuge in caves, trees and attics. Rarely harmful, bats are valuable in helping check insect populations.

LITTLE BROWN BAT
Myotis lucifugus
Size: 2-4 in. (5-10 cm)
Description: Small chocolate-brown bat with glossy fur.
Habitat: Variable throughout most of the state.
Comments: Alaska's most common and widespread bat, it is one of five species found here. Roosts in caves and buildings in small colonies during warmer months; the majority migrate south during winter.

RABBITS AND ALLIES

Most members of this distinctive group of mammals have long ears, large eyes and long hind legs. They commonly rest in protected areas like thickets during the day. When threatened, they thump their hind feet on the ground as an alarm signal.

Summer

Winter

SNOWSHOE HARE
Lepus americanus

Size: 18-20 in. (36-40 cm)
Description: Coat is brown to yellowish in summer and white in winter. Ears are black-tipped throughout the year. Large hind feet are well-furred to allow it to travel over deep snow.
Habitat: Mixed forests, thickets and wooded swamps throughout most of Alaska.
Comments: Also called the varying hare, it is most active at dusk and dawn. Feeds on grasses, buds, twigs and bark. The similar Arctic hare (*L. timidus*), found in western and northern Alaska is larger and has bigger ears.

COLLARED PIKA
Ochotona collaris

Size: 6-8 in. (15-20 cm)
Description: A small, rounded mammal with short legs and dark-ears. Fur is brown above and light below with a pale gray collar on the-neck and shoulders.
Habitat: Talus slopes.
Comments: It can be seen scurrying about rock piles gathering vegetation which it stores as 'hay' to feed on during winter months. Lives in small colonies. Short, shrill barking call serves to establish territory and warn of intruders.

SQUIRRELS AND ALLIES

This diverse family of hairy-tailed, large-eyed rodents includes chipmunks, tree squirrels, ground squirrels and marmots. Most are active during the day and easily observed in the field. The sizes noted include tail length.

RED SQUIRREL
Tamiasciurus hudsonicus

Size: 11-13 in. (28-33 cm)
Description: Rusty-olive squirrel has a whitish belly and underparts. Bushy tail is orangish.
Habitat: Forests throughout most of Alaska.
Comments: Active during the day, it is very vocal and often heard twittering and chattering. Feeds on seeds, berries and nuts. Spends much of the summer caching winter food stores.

NORTHERN FLYING SQUIRREL
Glaucomys sabrinus

Size: 12 in. (30 cm)
Description: Brown to cinnamon, large-eyed squirrel with a broad tail and a loose skin fold along its sides.
Habitat: Forested areas in central and southeastern Alaska.
Comments: Capable of gliding distances of over 100 ft. (30 m) by spreading its limbs and stretching its flight skin taut. A nocturnal species, it can be heard thumping about in the dark while foraging.

HOARY MARMOT
Marmota caligata

Size: 18-25 in. (46-64 cm)
Description: Large rodent has a grayish coat, black and white head and shoulders and dark feet and tail.
Habitat: Rocky mountain slopes.
Comments: Known for its shrill whistling call. The similar Alaskan marmot (*M. broweri*), found primarily in the Brooks Range, lacks a white face patch.

ARCTIC GROUND SQUIRREL
Spermophilus parryii

Size: 14-20 in. (36-51 cm)
Description: Tawny-colored squirrel has a gray-brown back covered with white flecks.
Habitat: Subalpine meadows, river valleys, moist and alpine tundra.
Comments: This highly vocal ground squirrel lives in large colonies in central and northern Alaska. It hibernates for more than half of the year from September-April.

BEAVERS

A single member of this family is found in North America. Beavers require 2-3 ft. (61-91 cm) of water in order to protect themselves from enemies. In areas where the water level is too low, they construct dams along waterways to flood the surrounding area. They either live in dens along the banks of waterways or in lodges incorporated into their dam.

BEAVER
Castor canadensis

Size: 3-4 ft. (.9-1.2 m)
Description: Large glossy brown rodent with a broad, flat, black tail.
Habitat: Found throughout forested parts of Alaska.
Comments: Tail is often slapped on the surface of the water as a warning signal. Active at dusk and dawn, they feed on bark, aquatic plants and grasses.

MICE AND ALLIES

Most members of this large group have rounded ears, long tails and
breed throughout the year.

DEER MOUSE
Peromyscus maniculatus

Size: 4-8 in. (10-20 cm)
Description: Bicolored coat is pale
gray to red-brown above and white
below. Long, hairy tail is
also bicolored.
Habitat: Common and widespread in a variety of habitats.
Comments: Feeds on seeds, buds, fruit
and wild plants. Active year-round.

NORTHERN RED-BACKED VOLE
Clethrionomys rutilus

Size: 4-6 in. (10-15 cm)
Description: Fuzzy, mouse-like
rodent has gray-brown sides
and a reddish back.
Habitat: Damp forests and meadows.
Comments: Often scurries about
under ground cover and is
difficult to observe. Active
throughout the year, they tunnel
through the snow in winter. One of
seven species of vole found in Alaska.

MUSKRAT
Ondatra zibethica

Size: 10-14 in. (26-36 cm)
Description: Often mistaken
for beavers, these aquatic rodents
are smaller and have a long, scaly
tail that is flattened on either side.
Habitat: Marshes, lakes, waterways.
Comments: In swampy areas, they
construct dome-shaped houses of
marsh vegetation up to 3 ft. (.9 m)
high. Feeds primarily on aquatic
plants. Active year-round.

BROWN LEMMING
Lemmus sibricus

Size: 25-40 in. (64-102 cm)
Description: Rounded, heavily-furred, brownish rodent has a stubby tail.
Habitat: Wet tundra, alpine meadows.
Comments: Lemmings are active throughout the year and are an extremely important food source for other animals. When populations peak every 3-5 years, they often undergo a frenzied migration to find new food sources. Five species are found in Alaska.

PORCUPINES

Porcupines are medium-sized mammals with coats of stiff, barbed quills. When threatened, they face away from their aggressor, erect the quills and lash out with their tail. The loosely rooted quills detach on contact and are extremely difficult to remove.

PORCUPINE
Erethizon dorsatum

Size: 25-35 in. (64-89 cm)
Description: Distinguished by its chunky profile, arched back and long coat of barbed quills.
Habitat: Forested areas and tall shrub thickets.
Comments: Spends much of its time in spruce and hemlock trees feeding on leaves, twigs and bark. Active throughout the year.

WEASELS AND ALLIES

Members of this group have prominent anal scent glands which are used for social and sexual communication.

SHORT-TAILED WEASEL
Mustela erminea

Size: 9-15 in. (20-38 cm)
Description: Long-bodied mammal has short legs and a black-tipped tail. Coat is brown above, white below in summer, and all-white in winter.
Habitat: Variable.
Comments: Also called ermine. The similar least weasel (*M. rixosa)* is smaller (6-8 in./15-20 cm).

MINK
Mustela vison

Size: 20-25 in. (51-64 cm)
Description: Coat is typically chocolate brown with irregular white patches on the chin, throat and belly.
Habitat: Near water.
Comments: Highly aquatic, they den along waterways and feed on fish, amphibians, crustaceans and small mammals. Mink are abundant in southeastern Alaska.

MARTEN
Martes americana

Size: 23-26 in. (58-66 cm)
Description: Coat is yellow-brown to dark brown with a pale buff patch on the neck and chest.
Habitat: Mature forests.
Comments: Active at night, they feed on rodents, berries, birds and fish. Also called 'sable,' its coat is highly valued by trappers.

WOLVERINE
Gulo gulo

Size: 35-42 in. (89-107 cm)
Description: Stout and bear-like, it has a long brown to black coat with broad light stripes on either side.
Habitat: Forests and tundra, remote alpine wilderness.
Comments: Also known as 'devil bear,' it is renowned for its fierce temperament. An opportunistic omnivore, it feeds on whatever it can kill or find.

RIVER OTTER
Lutra canadensis

Size: 40-50 in. (1-1.3 m)
Description: Sleek long-bodied mammal has a glossy gray-brown coat, thick tail and webbed hind feet.
Habitat: Near water throughout most of Alaska.
Comments: Hunts on land and in fresh and saltwater where it feeds on fishes, amphibians, crustaceans and small mammals. Fond of play, they often make slides along riverbanks in mud or snow.

SEA OTTER
Enhydra lutris

Size: 30-60 in. (.75-1.5 m)
Description: Similar to the river otter, it inhabits only saltwater and has a yellowish face.
Habitat: Kelp beds near rocky coasts.
Comments: Spends much of its time at sea eating and sleeping while floating on its back. Often uses a stone to break open sea urchins and shellfish when feeding.

DOGS

Members of this family have long snouts, erect ears and resemble domestic dogs in looks and habit. All are active year-round.

ARCTIC FOX
Alopex lagopus

Size: 40-45 in. (101-114 cm)
Description: Coat is white in winter and brownish in summer. A blue variant found chiefly in the Aleutian Islands and western Alaska remains charcoal-colored year-round.
Habitat: Forests, tundra.
Comments: Often spotted along the coasts of western and northern Alaska; may venture onto pack ice in winter.

RED FOX
Vulpes vulpes

Size: 40-55 in. (1-1.4 m)
Description: Small, rusty-reddish dog has a bushy, white-tipped tail and dark stockings. Black and silver variants also occur, all of which can be distinguished by their white-tipped tail.
Habitat: Damp tundra, lowlands, open areas.
Comments: Feeds on lemmings, voles, squirrels, hares, birds and insects and will often cache excess food when it is plentiful.

GRAY WOLF
Canis lupus

Size: 55-70 in. (1.4-1.8 m)
Description: Distinguished from other dogs by its large size. Coat color is variable, with gray and black wolves the most common.
Habitat: Forests, tundra, wilderness areas throughout 85% of the state.
Comments: Highly social animals, they live and hunt in packs of between 2 and 30 animals.

CATS

These highly specialized carnivores are renowned hunters. All have short faces, keen vision, powerful bodies and retractable claws. Most are nocturnal hunters.

LYNX
Felis lynx

Size: 3-3.5 ft. (.9-1.1 m)
Description: Large cat is distinguished by its large feet, tufted ears and short, black-tipped tail.
Habitat: Variable throughout Alaska.
Comments: A nocturnal hunter, it feeds primarily on hares. Its thickly furred feet act like snowshoes in the winter.

BEARS

This group includes the largest terrestrial carnivores in the world. All are heavy-bodied, large-headed animals, with short ears and small tails. Their sense of smell is keen, though eyesight is generally poor. Key places to view bears are listed in the section on natural attractions.

BLACK BEAR
Ursus americanus

Size: 4-5 ft. (1.2-1.5 m)
Description: Coat is normally black, but brown and cinnamon variants are also found in the south. A rare blue (glacier) phase occurs in the southeast.
Habitat: Forested areas south of the Brooks Range.
Comments: Diet consists of berries, vegetation, fish, insects, mammals and refuse. Its tracks can sometimes be spotted in muddy areas near water.

BROWN BEAR
Ursus arctos

Size: 6-9 ft. (1.8-2.7 m)
Description: Distinguished by its large size, prominent shoulder hump and huge feet with prominent claws.
Habitat: Open habitats and forested areas throughout most of the state excluding the southeasternmost islands.
Comments: Three subspecies of brown bear are found in Alaska. One group lives in coastal areas and feeds primarily on salmon. A second, group (often called 'grizzlies') are found in inland and northern habitats; these are typically smaller since they have less protein in their diet. A third group found on Kodiak Island are classified as a separate subspecies since they are physically isolated. The huge Kodiak Island brown bears are considered the largest land carnivores in the world. Though the polar bear (*U. maritimus*) is larger still, it is considered a marine mammal.

HOOFED MAMMALS

This general grouping includes hoofed mammals from a variety of families.

SITKA BLACK-TAILED DEER
Odocoileus hemionus sitkensis

Size: 5 ft. (1.5 m)
Description: Small deer has a coat that is red-brown in summer and grayish in winter. Tail is black on top.
Habitat: Coastal rainforests.
Comments: Recent transplants have established populations in south-central and southwestern Alaska.

CARIBOU
Rangifer tarandus

Size: 6-9 ft. (1.8-2.7 m)
Description: Distinguished by its large antlers, shaggy brown neck and light rump patch. They have large concave hooves that spread widely to support it on snow and soft tundra.
Habitat: Tundra, muskeg, forests.
Comments: Caribou are the only member of the deer family in which both sexes grow antlers. There are about a million caribou in Alaska. Herds numbering up to 350,000 animals travel up to 900 miles during annual migration from summer calving areas to wintering grounds.

DALL SHEEP
Ovis dalli

Size: 4-5 ft. (1.2-1.5 m)
Description: Coat is white with a yellowish cast. Males have massive coiled horns.
Habitat: Mountainous areas.
Comments: Both sexes have horns but the male's are much larger. Males are noted for their spectacular head-butting contests which serve to establish dominance.

MOOSE
Alces alces

Size: 7-9 ft. (2.1-2.7 m)
Description: Huge, horse-sized animal with long, thin legs and a pendulous snout. Males have enormous, flattened antlers and a prominent neck 'bell' of skin and hair.
Habitat: Forests near shallow lakes, rivers and swamps.
Comments: Largely solitary animals, they are most active at dawn and dusk. Females with young can be very aggressive and should be avoided.

MOUNTAIN GOAT
Oreamnos americanus

Size: 4-6 ft. (1.2-1.8 m)
Description: Distinguished by its long, shaggy white coat and black, dagger-like horns.
Habitat: Remote mountainous areas.
Comments: They are found in high alpine meadows in summer and near the treeline in winter. Transplanted populations have also been established on a few islands.

MUSKOX
Ovibos moschatus

Size: 6-8 ft. (1.8-2.4 m)
Description: Stocky, long-haired cow-like creature with wraparound horns.
Habitat: Tundra and foothills.
Comments: When threatened, they protect their young by forming circles around them and facing outward. Like Dall sheep, the males engage in spectacular head-butting contests to establish dominance. The native population was exterminated by hunters in the 1800s. Animals were reintroduced from Greenland in the 1930s and several thousand exist today in the wild. A domesticated herd is found in Palmer.

MARINE MAMMALS

This group includes a variety of mammals that live in or on the water. Seals and their kin live in water and breed on land. The fish-like dolphins and whales spend all their time in the water, breathing air through blowholes set high on their heads. Unlike fish, marine mammals with fins have tails with horizontal, rather than vertical, flukes.

POLAR BEAR
Ursus maritimus

Size: 7-11 ft. (2.1-3.4 m)
Description: Huge white bear. Coat often has yellowish tinge.
Habitat: Sea ice, ocean shores.
Comments: Polar bears are considered marine mammals since they spend the majority of their life on floating sea ice. They are most closely related to brown bears and the two species have mated successfully in zoos. They remain active throughout the year and feed primarily on seals and other marine mammals. Pregnant females create dens on sea ice or on land and hibernate November-March. Males are active year-round.

PACIFIC WALRUS
Odobenus rosmarus

Size: 8-12 ft. (2.4-3.7 m)
Description: Distinguished at a glance by its large size, wrinkled skin and large ivory tusks.
Habitat: Found seasonally on polar islands between Bristol Bay and Point Barrow. Winters on pack ice.
Comments: The tusks are used as tools for fighting, climbing and chopping. Feeds primarily on clams and shellfish. Adult bulls can weigh up to 4,000 lbs. (1,814 kg).

NORTHERN SEA LION
Eumetopias jubatus

Size: 7-10 ft. (2.1-3 m)
Description: Coat is yellow-brown above, red-brown below. Males have enlarged necks and shoulders, a 'mane' of coarse hair and are up to 3 times the size of females.
Habitat: Rocky shores and coastal waters.
Comments: Large numbers gather seasonally to pup and breed on well-defined, traditionally-used rookeries. About 70% of the world's population of northern sea lions reside in Alaskan waters.

HARBOR SEAL
Phoca vitulina

Size: 4-6 ft. (1.2-1.8 m)
Description: Coat is dark-colored with light rings, or light-colored with dark blotches. Also called 'leopard seal.'
Habitat: Coastal waters, harbors, bays, occasionally in rivers and lakes.
Comments: Found basking along shorelines at all times of the day, often in large groups. Numbers are present at Iliamna Lake year-round.

PACIFIC WHITE-SIDED DOLPHIN
Lagenorhynchus obliquidens

Size: 6-8 ft. (1.8-2.4 m)
Description: Dark above, light below with pale side stripes and a white belly.
Habitat: Spotted near shorelines in winter and spring.
Comments: Travels in large herds of up to several thousand. Feeds primarily on small fish and squid.

HARBOR PORPOISE
Phocoena phocoena

Size: 4-6 ft. (1.2-1.8 m)
Description: Dull-colored porpoise is dark gray above and light-colored below.
Habitat: Nearshore waters.
Comments: Commonly spotted in coastal waters. Ranges from Alaska to Mexico.

DALL'S PORPOISE
Phocoenoides dalli

Size: 5-6 ft. (1.5-1.8 m)
Description: Resembling a miniature killer whale, it is told by its black body and large white belly patch.
Habitat: Common in coastal waters.
Comments: Found in groups of 2 to 20 individuals. Often plays around ships. Porpoises are generally distinguished from dolphins by their shorter snouts and stockier bodies.

BELUGA WHALE
Delphinapterus leucas

Size: 10-15 ft. (3-4.6 m)
Description: Small whale has a small head and a bulging forehead. Adult whales are white; young whales are brownish and lighten in color as they mature.
Habitat: Coastal waters, shallow bays.
Comments: Also called the 'sea canary' it produces a vast repertoire of whistles, grunts and clicks used to navigate, find prey and communicate. They will often ascend rivers and have been spotted several hundred miles from the sea.

HUMPBACK WHALE
Megaptera novaeangliae

Size: 40-50 ft. (12-15 m)
Description: Dark whale has a humped back, and very long flippers with scalloped edges. Underside of flippers and flukes is white.
Habitat: Coastal during migration.
Comments: Frequently observed close to shore along the southern coast of Alaska. Feeds primarily on small schooling fish like herring.

GRAY WHALE
Eschrichtius robustus

Size: 36-50 ft. (10-15 m)
Description: Large, mottled gray-blue whale has a small dorsal hump and 2-5 throat grooves. Skin is often blotched with abrasions, scars and parasitic barnacles which cluster on its head and back.
Habitat: Abundant in coastal waters during winter-spring migration.
Comments: Often observed in large numbers along Alaskan shores. A baleen whale, it has a sieve-like structure in its mouth that strains small crustaceans, fish and plankton from the water.

BOWHEAD WHALE
Balaena mysticetus

Size: 40-60 ft. (12-18 m)
Description: Large, robust whale has a highly arched jaw. Its mouth and head comprise 1/4–1/3 of its body length.
Habitat: North Pacific and Arctic oceans.
Comments: An important subsistence animal for many of Alaska's northwestern coastal natives. It is

the only whale to spend its entire life in Arctic waters and has a layer of blubber up to 1.5 ft (.46 m) thick.

Alaska's State Marine Mammal

KILLER WHALE
Orcinus orca

Size: 15-30 ft. (4.5-9 m)
Description: Told by jet-black body, white belly and white eye spots.
Habitat: Throughout Alaskan waters.
Comments: Known as 'sea wolves,' killer whales travel in groups of up to 40 individuals and hunt as a pack when attacking large whales. They are opportunistic carnivores and will feed on virtually any large marine animal. They have even been observed snatching seals and sea lions from shore. A member of the dolphin family, it is called a whale because of its large size.

WHAT ARE BIRDS?

Birds are warm-blooded, feathered animals with two wings and two legs. The majority can fly and adaptations for flight include hollow bones and an enhanced breathing capacity. Birds also have an efficient four-chambered heart and are insulated against the weather to enhance temperature regulation.

HOW TO IDENTIFY BIRDS

The best way to become good at identifying birds is simply to practice. The more birds you attempt to identify, the better you'll become at distinguishing species.

When birding, the first thing to note is the habitat you are exploring in order to know what kinds of birds to expect. When you spot a bird, check for obvious field marks. Note the shape of its silhouette and beak. Note the color and pattern of its feathers for distinguishing markings at rest and in flight. Is it small (sparrow), medium (crow), or large (heron)? Does it have any unusual behavioral characteristics?

If you are interested in enhancing your field skills, it is essential to become familiar with bird songs. It is often difficult to positively iden- tify birds by sight in dense cover or poor light and many species are easily distinguished by their call. Bird song tapes and CDs are available from nature stores and libraries.

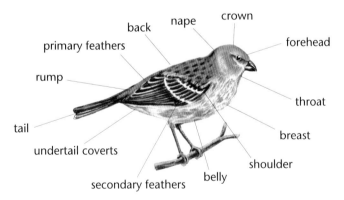

N.B. – *It is important to note that many species illustrations feature the adult male in its breeding coloration. Colors and markings shown may be duller or absent during different times of the year.*

LOONS

These stout-bodied birds have long necks and pointed bills. Excellent swimmers, they can dive over 250 ft. (76 m) in search of fish. When alarmed they will often dive, rather then fly, to safety. Five species are found in Alaska.

COMMON LOON
Gavia immer

Size: 32 in. (81 cm)
Description: Distinguished by its black head and checkered and spotted back.
Habitat: Lakes in summer, southern coast in winter.
Comments: Noted for their resonant, haunting call – *ha-oo, ha-oo, ha-oo* – often heard at dusk.

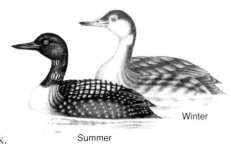

Winter

Summer

RED-THROATED LOON
Gavia stellata

Size: 25 in. (64 cm)
Description: Gray loon with a red throat patch and vertical white and black stripes on its nape.
Habitat: Lakes and arctic coast in summer, southern coast in winter.
Comments: The pacific loon (*G. pacifica*) has a gray head and nape and a black throat patch.

GREBES

The members of this group of duck-like birds have short tails, slender necks and stiff bills. Excellent divers, they have lobed toes rather than webbed feet and their legs are located near the back of the body to help propel them through the water.

RED-NECKED GREBE
Podiceps grisegena

Size: 19 in. (48 cm)
Description: Distinguished in summer by its red neck, white cheek and chin and black cap. Winter adults are grayish with white crescents on their heads.
Habitat: Lakes and ponds in summer, southern coast in winter.
Comments: Hatchlings are often carried and fed on the backs of their parents. One of four species of grebe found in Alaska.

Winter

Summer

CORMORANTS

Large black seabirds are often spotted perched on rocks along the coast.

DOUBLE-CRESTED CORMORANT
Phalacrocorax auritus

Size: 30-36 in. (76-90 cm)
Description: This large black bird is distinguished by its slender neck, hooked bill and orange throat patch. Often perches with its wings spread to let them dry. Head crests are rarely evident.
Habitat: Common in coastal waters, some found inland.
Comments: Cormorants nest in colonies on rocky ledges. Two other similar species are found in Alaska.

HERON-LIKE BIRDS

Large wading birds with long legs, long necks and slender bills. Though similar-looking, herons and cranes belong to different orders of birds.

GREAT BLUE HERON
Ardea herodias

Size: 40-52 in. (1-1.3 m)
Description: Large, slender bluish bird with long legs, a long, yellowish bill and white face. Black plumes extend back from the eye.
Habitat: Coastal waters in south-central and southeast Alaska.
Comments: Often seen stalking fish in shallow water.

SANDHILL CRANE
Grus canadensis

Size: 45 in. (1.1 m)
Description: Tall, slender, gray to brown bird with a red forehead patch, black legs and a black, chisel-like bill.
Habitat: Nests on tundra, marshes, muskegs.
Comments: Two distinct populations are found in northern and southern Alaska. Noted for its mating dance of deep bows followed by leaps, skips and turns.

SWANS

Large white, long-necked waterfowl are graceful in the water and the air.

TUNDRA SWAN
Cygnus columbianus

Size: 48-55 in. (1.2-1.4 m)
Description: Large all-white bird has a black bill with a yellow spot near the eye. (Spot not always evident.)
Habitat: Near marshes, ponds, lakes and rivers.
Comments: Formerly called the whistling swan. Distinguished from the similar-looking, larger trumpeter swan (*C. buccinator*) by its call; the tundra swan has a high, whooping call, while the trumpeter has a low, horn-like call.

GEESE

Geese are highly terrestrial birds often spotted grazing near water. Noisy in flight, they are often heard before they're seen passing overhead.

CANADA GOOSE
Branta canadensis

Size: 24-40 in. (60-102 cm)
Description: Told by black head and neck, and white cheek patch.
Habitat: Near marshes, ponds, lakes and rivers in summer.
Comments: Geese fly in a 'V' formation when migrating. Pairs usually mate for life. Call is a nasal *honk*. Six of the 10 subspecies of Canada geese are found in Alaska.

WHITE-FRONTED GOOSE
Anser albifrons

Size: 18-22 in. (46-56 cm)
Description: Brownish goose is distinguished by its pink bill and orange legs.
Habitat: Tundra lakes, ponds and rivers in summer.
Comments: Common name refers to the patch of white feathers at the bill base. Several hundred thousand nest in Alaska each year.

EMPEROR GOOSE
Chen canagica

Size: 16-20 in. (41-51 cm)
Description: Chunky, bluish-gray bird has feathers edged in black and white. Note its yellow feet, black throat and white tail.
Habitat: Most nest in the Yukon Delta region and winter in south-western and southcentral Alaska.
Comments: Rarely found far from marine waters, they are also called beach geese.

BRANT GOOSE
Branta bernicla

Size: 22-26 in. (56-66 cm)
Description: Small goose with a black head and neck and a white 'necklace.'
Habitat: The majority nest in the Yukon Delta region.
Comments: A huge concentration gathers annually at the Izembek National Wildlife Refuge between August and October.

DUCKS AND ALLIES

Smaller than geese, ducks have shorter necks and are primarily aquatic. In most, breeding males are more brightly colored than females. Both sexes have a brightly-colored band (speculum) on the trailing edge of the wing.

MALLARD
Anas platyrhynchos

Size: 20-28 in. (51-71 cm)
Description: Male has green head, white collar and chestnut breast. Female is mottled brown. Both have a metallic blue speculum.
Habitat: Ponds and marshes.
Comments: The ancestor of domestic ducks. Call is a loud *quack*.

NORTHERN PINTAIL
Anas acuta

Size: 20-30 in. (51-76 cm)
Description: Distinguished by its
long neck and pointed tail.
Male has a white breast
and a white neck stripe.
Both sexes have a glossy
brown speculum bordered in white.
Habitat: Marshes and ponds.
Comments: Likely the most abun-
dant and widespread duck in Alaska.

GREEN-WINGED TEAL
Anas crecca

Size: 12-15 in. (30-38 cm)
Description: Male has a
chestnut head and a
green eye patch. Female
is brown-gray. Both have
a bright green speculum.
Habitat: Ponds and lakes in
summer.
Comments: One of the earliest
spring migrants to appear. Feeds
by dabbling in shallow water.
Call is a clear, short whistle.

NORTHERN SHOVELER
Anas clypeata

Size: 17-20 in. (43-50 cm)
Description: Told by its flat
head and large, spatulate bill.
Male has a green head, rusty
sides and a blue wing patch.
Habitat: Marshes, ponds and
lakes in summer.
Comments: Shovel-shaped bill is
used to strain aquatic animals and
vegetation from the water. Swims
with bill pointed downward.

BUFFLEHEAD
Bucephala albeola

Size: 12-16 in. (15-20 cm)
Description: Small, puffy-headed duck. Male is distinguished by the large white patch on its iridescent, black head. Female is gray-brown with a white cheek patch.
Habitat: Inland lakes and rivers in summer, coastal waters in winter.
Comments: A diving duck, it feeds on fishes, crustaceans and mollusks.

GREATER SCAUP
Aythya marila

Size: 16-20 in. (41-51 cm)
Description: Chunky duck with a glossy, dark head, gray back and white flanks.
Habitat: Deep ponds and sloughs in summer, southern coast in winter.
Comments: Very similar to the lesser scaup (*A. affinis*) which is slightly smaller and has a different head shape and bill size.

OLDSQUAW
Clangula hyemalis

Size: 16-23 in. (41-58 cm)
Description: Distinctive light and dark-patterned duck with a long tail. Female is mottled and lacks long tail.
Habitat: Tundra lakes and sloughs in summer, southern coast in winter.
Comments: The males' yodeling calls can be heard in protected coastal bays in winter.

HARLEQUIN DUCK
Histrionicus histrionicus

Size: 15-19 in. (38-48 cm)
Description: Compact, colorful
duck has bluish plumage with
bold white markings on its head
and breast.
Habitat: Inland rivers and streams
in summer, southern coast in winter.
Comments: Feeds on a wide variety
of invertebrates and small fish. Often
spotted perching along rocky coasts.

COMMON GOLDENEYE
Bucephala clangula

Size: 15-20 in. (38-51 cm)
Description: Male is distinguished
by its glossy green head and white
patch below its eye. Mottled gray
female has a tawny head.
Habitat: Lakes and ponds in
summers, southern coastal
waters in winter.
Comments: Nests in tree cavities.
The male of the similar Barrow's
goldeneye (*B. islandica*) has a dark
purplish head and a white crescent
below its eye.

COMMON EIDER
Somateria mollisima

Size: 24 in. (61 cm)
Description: Black-capped male
has a white chest and back and
a black rump and sides.
Habitat: Coastal waters.
Comments: Holds head below
body in flight. Most winter in
the Aleutian Islands and on
the Bering Sea.

KING EIDER
Somateria spectabilis

Size: 23 in. (57 cm)
Description: Males are distinguished at a glance by their red bill and large, orangish frontal lobe that extends from the bill to the forehead.
Habitat: Northern coastal waters.
Comments: Up to one million king eiders migrate through the Beaufort Sea annually. About 10,000 breed in Alaska.

WHITE-WINGED SCOTER
Melanitta fusca

Size: 20-24 in. (51-61 cm)
Description: Black male has a swollen bill and white eye and wing patches. Females are brownish with white wing patches and two light facial markings.
Habitat: Lakes and ponds in summer, southern coast in winter.
Comments: The male surf scoter (*M. perspicillata*) lacks a white eye patch and has white patches on its nape and forehead.

HAWKS, EAGLES AND ALLIES

Primarily carnivorous, these birds have sharp talons for grasping prey and sharply hooked bills for tearing into flesh. Many soar on wind currents when hunting. Sexes are similar in most.

SHARP-SHINNED HAWK
Accipiter striatus

Size: 12 in. (30 cm)
Description: Plumage is gray above and light below. Underparts are barred with brownish-orange stripes. Females tend to be browner than males.
Habitat: Forests.
Comments: The sharp-shinned hawk has short, rounded wings that enable it to maneuver through dense woods in search of prey. It feeds primarily on small mammals and songbirds.

RED-TAILED HAWK
Buteo jamaicensis
Size: 20-25 in. (51-64 cm)
Description: Dark, broad-winged, wide-tailed hawk with light under-parts and a red tail. A dark belly band is often evident in flight.
Habitat: Forests in central and southern Alaska in summer.
Comments: Eats primarily small mammals and other birds.

BALD EAGLE
Haliaeetus leucocephalus
Size: 30-40 in. (76-102 cm)
Description: Large brown bird with a white head and tail.
Habitat: Throughout southern coastal Alaska year-round, inland lakes and forests in summer.
Comments: Distinctive plumage is not attained for several years; young birds are brown and are easily con-fused with golden eagles. Thousands congregate to feed on spawning salmon in the Chilkat Valley in autumn and early winter.

GOLDEN EAGLE
Aquila chrysaetos
Size: 30-40 in. (76-102 cm)
Description: Large, dark soaring bird has long, broad wings. It is distinguished from hawks by its large size.
Habitat: Mountainous regions, remote forests.
Comments: Feeds on mammals, some birds and carrion. Most common in central Alaska.

PEREGRINE FALCON
Falco peregrinus
Size: 15-20 in. (38-51 cm)
Description: Plumage is blue-gray above and light below. Note dark sideburn on cheek and barred chest.
Habitat: Open country, river valleys in summer, southern coast in winter.
Comments: Three subspecies of peregrine falcon are found in Alaska, two of which are endangered. Spectacular fliers, they prey on birds they capture on the wing.

CHICKEN-LIKE BIRDS

Ground-dwelling birds that are chicken-like in looks and habit. Most have stout bills, rounded wings and heavy bodies. Primarily ground-dwelling, they are capable of short bursts of flight.

Ruffed

Blue

SPRUCE GROUSE
Dendrapagus canadensis
Size: 12-18 in. (31-46 cm)
Description: Dark male has black chin and breast and red eye combs. Female is brownish. Most have a band of rusty brown at the tail tip; those found in southeast Alaska lack this band and have white-tipped feathers at the tail base.
Habitat: Spruce-hardwood forests.
Comments: Prefer forests with an understory of berry bushes. Common in central and northern Alaska.

RUFFED GROUSE
Bonasa umbellus
Size: 16-19 in. (41-48 cm)
Description: Red or gray grouse with a small head crest and broad, black band near the tail tip. Note dark ruffs on the side of the neck.
Habitat: Mixed forests.
Comments: Males advertise for mates in the spring by perching on fallen logs and loudly 'drumming' the air with their wings. In southeastern Alaska, blue grouse (*Dendrapagus obscurus*) males can be heard attracting females with a loud, hooting display.

WILLOW PTARMIGAN
Lagopus lagopus

Size: 12-17 in. (31-43 cm)
Description: Small, chunky birds
have feathered toes. In summer,
males are red-brown above and white
below; females are mottled brown.
Both are all-white in winter
except for black tails.
Habitat: Alpine and arctic tundra.
Comments: Active throughout the
year, they feed on insects, berries,
seeds and buds. One of three species
of ptarmigan found in Alaska.

Alaska's State Bird

SHOREBIRDS

These birds are normally found along shores of oceans, lakes and ponds.
Most have slender bills which they use to probe in sand and mud for
invertebrates. This general grouping includes several distinct families of
birds.

SEMI-PALMATED PLOVER
Charadrius semipalmatus

Size: 7 in. (18 cm)
Description: Brown shorebird with a
white breast, a single black neck
band and an orange, black-tipped,
pigeon-like bill.
Habitat: Southern coastal areas; nests
in barren areas and along beaches.
Comments: Adults will call inces-
santly if nesting area is approached.

BLACK-BELLIED PLOVER
Pluvialis squatarola

Size: 11-15 in. (28-38 cm)
Description: Told by whitish crown
and neck stripe, black face and belly
and white undertail coverts.
Habitat: Mudflats, tundra and coastal
shores in summer.
Comments: Feeds by tilting forward,
taking a few steps, and tilting forward again. The similar-looking
American golden plover
(*P. dominicus*) is smaller and has
black undertail coverts.

Greater   Lesser

GREATER YELLOWLEGS
Tringa melanoleuca
Size: 14 in. (36 cm)

LESSER YELLOWLEGS
Tringa flavipes
Size: 10 in. (25 cm)

Description: Distinguished from other shorebirds by their large size and long, bright yellow legs. The greater yellowlegs is taller and has a thicker bill that may be upturned slightly.
Habitat: Coastal wetlands, lake and pond margins.
Comments: The calls of the two species are distinctive; the greater has a descending three- to four-note call (*kyew, kyew, kyew*), while the lesser's is one- or two-notes (*tu, tu*).

SPOTTED SANDPIPER
Actitis macularia

Size: 6-8 in. (15-20 cm)
Description: Small brown bird with light, dark-spotted underparts and spindly, yellowish legs. Spots are evident during breeding season.
Habitat: Southern coastal areas, lakes, and rivers in summer.
Comments: A solitary bird, it teeters back and forth when walking. Flies with quivering wings held downward, alternating with low glides.

LEAST SANDPIPER
Calidris minutilla

Size: 5-7 in. (13-18 cm)
Description: A small brownish bird with a short, thin bill and yellowish legs.
Habitat: Tundra, meadows, and muskegs in summer.
Comments: A very common shorebird, it often crouches to feed. Call is a high *peep*.

WESTERN SANDPIPER
Calidris mauri

Size: 6-7 in. (15-18 cm)
Description: Key field marks are black legs and rusty patches on crown, ear and shoulder. Bill is long and droops slightly at the tip.
Habitat: Tundra, mudflats and coastal areas in summer.
Comments: There are dozens of similar species of sandpiper that are difficult to distinguish in the field. Some birders refer to them as 'LBJs' or 'little brown jobs.'

DUNLIN
Calidris alpina

Size: 8-9 in. (20-23 cm)
Description: Distinguished from other sandpipers by its rusty back, black belly and long bill which droops at the tip. Belly is white in winter.
Habitat: Tundra, marshes, ponds and tidal areas.
Comments: Often occurs in flocks of thousands. The bulk of the entire population passes through the Copper River Delta in spring.

RED-NECKED PHALAROPE
Phalaropus lobatus

Size: 6-8 in. (15-20 cm)
Description: A small grayish bird with a white throat and belly. Female has a reddish neck patch; male's is brown.
Habitat: Coastal marshes, muskegs, small ponds and lakes.
Comments: Over a million nest throughout north and central Alaska. The similar red phalarope (*P. fulicaria*) has a yellow bill and is also abundant and common in coastal marshes. Unlike most shorebirds, they spend much time swimming in open water.

COMMON SNIPE
Gallinago gallinago

Size: 10-12 in. (25-30 cm)
Description: Stocky, long-billed shorebird with a spotted breast and streaked back.
Habitat: Coastal wetlands and muskegs.
Comments: When flushed it gives a sharp cry and flies off erratically. Male is noted for its spectacular courtship ritual.

BLACK OYSTERCATCHER
Haematopus bachmani

Size: 15-20 in. (38-51 cm)
Description: Black shorebird with a red bill and pink legs.
Habitat: Rocky sea shores.
Comments: The stout bill is used to pry and break open shellfish. Call is a piercing whistle.

GULL-LIKE BIRDS

Typically gray and white birds found near water. Representatives of three distinct families are included in this category

GLAUCOUS-WINGED GULL
Larus glaucescens

Size: 24-27 in. (61-69 cm)
Description: Large gull is distinguished by its large, red-spotted bill, dark eyes and pink legs.
Habitat: Coastal areas throughout southern and western Alaska.
Comments: The similar, yellow-eyed glaucous gull (*L. hyperboreus*) is found throughout Alaska.

HERRING GULL
Larus argentatus

Size: 22-26 in. (56-66 cm)
Description: Key field marks are white-spotted, black wing tips, yellow eyes and pink legs.
Habitat: Lakes, rivers, garbage dumps.
Comments: The only large gull that is common inland. The similar-looking mew gull (*L. brachyrhynchos*) is smaller (15-17 in./38-43 cm).

BONAPARTE'S GULL
Larus philadelphia

Size: 12-14 in. (30-36 cm)
Description: Small, black-headed gull with reddish legs.
Habitat: Near lakes, rivers and muskegs in summer.
Comments: Often found in the company of terns. Named for Napoleon's nephew, an ornithologist.

BLACK-LEGGED KITTIWAKE
Rissa tridactyla

Size: 16 in. (41 cm)
Description: This gull-like bird is distinguished by its black legs and solid black (dipped-in-ink) wing tips.
Habitat: Coastal cliffs in summer, open ocean in winter.
Comments: The similar red-legged kittiwake (*R. brevirostris*), has bright red legs.

ARCTIC TERN
Sterna paradisaea

Size: 14-16 in. (36-41 cm)
Description: Distinguished by its black cap, red bill and long, forked tail.
Habitat: Lakes, rivers and coastal areas in summer.
Comments: Winters as far south as Antarctica, an annual migration of over 22,000 miles (35,404 km). One of four species of tern found in Alaska.

LONG-TAILED JAEGER
Stercorarius longicaudus

Size: 20-23 in. (51-58 cm)
Description: Tern-like bird with pointed wings and long tail feathers.
Habitat: Tundra in summer, open ocean in winter.
Comments: Preys on lemmings, mice, insects and fish. One of three species of jaeger found in Alaska.

PUFFINS AND ALLIES

These stubby birds all have short necks, short, pointed wings and webbed feet.

HORNED PUFFIN
Fratecula corniculata

Size: 12-14 in. (30-36 cm)
Description: Parrot-like, black and white bird with a white belly and a large orange bill. Fleshy dark 'horn' is found above each eye.
Habitat: Coastal islands in summer, open sea in winter.
Comments: Feeds on fish which it 'flys' after underwater. The similar tufted puffin (*F. cirrhata),* also found in Alaska, has a black belly and prominent tufts of golden feathers that curl back from each side of its head.

PIGEON GUILLEMOT
Cepphus columba

Size: 12-14 in. (30-36 cm)
Description: Small black seabird with a conspicuous white patch on each wing.
Habitat: Coastal islands in summer, open sea in winter.
Comments: Like puffins, they 'fly' underwater in pursuit of fish.

MARBLED MURRELET
Brachyramphus marmoratus

Size: 8-10 in. (20-25 cm)
Description: Small seabird is
brown above and mottled
white below.
Habitat: Coastal in summer,
open sea in winter.
Comments: Nests in trees, often
several miles inland. Feeds on
fish and marine invertebrates.

COMMON MURRE
Uria aalge

Size: 15-19 in. (38-48 cm)
Description: This duck-sized bird is
black above and white below. Note
slender bill.
Habitat: Coastal in summer, open sea
in winter.
Comments: The similar-looking
thick-billed murre (*U. lomvia*), has a
white mark on its black bill.

DOVES

These familiar birds feed largely on seeds, grain and insects.

ROCK DOVE
Columba livia

Size: 12-14 in. (30-36 cm)
Description: Blue-gray bird with a
white rump and black-banded tail.
White, tan and brown variants also
exist.
Habitat: Common in urban areas.
Comments: This introduced species is
relatively tame and can be trained for
homing.

OWLS

These square-shaped birds of prey have large heads, large eyes and hooked bills. Sexes are similar.

GREAT HORNED OWL
Bubo virginianus

Size: 20-25 in. (51-64 cm)
Description: Large, dark brown bird with prominent ear tufts, yellow eyes and a white throat.
Habitat: Forests.
Comments: Primarily nocturnal, it feeds on small mammals and birds. Sometimes spotted hunting during the day. Voice is a deep, resonant *hoo-hoo-hooooo.*

SHORT-EARED OWL
Asio flammeus

Size: 12-16 in. (30-41 cm)
Description: Small owl with a rounded head and heavily streaked breast.
Habitat: Tundra, wetlands, muskegs and open areas in summer.
Comments: Often spotted in early evening flying low over fields and marshes in search of prey. Nests on the ground.

SNOWY OWL
Nyctea scandiaca

Size: 20-25 in. (51-64 cm)
Description: Large white owl. Breast and wings have a variable amount of black barring.
Habitat: Tundra, marshes.
Comments: Often hunts during the day. When food is scarce in winter, many migrate south.

HUMMINGBIRDS

The smallest birds, hummingbirds are named for the noise made by their wings during flight. All have long needle-like bills and long tongues which are used to extract nectar from flowers.

RUFOUS HUMMINGBIRD
Selasphorus rufus

Size: 3-4 in. (8-10 cm)
Description: Small, red-brown hummingbird. Female is greenish above, and red-brown below.
Habitat: Urban areas, thickets, alpine meadows.
Comments: Alaska's only common hummingbird, it nests in southeast and southcentral areas. Migrates to Mexico in winter.

KINGFISHERS

Solitary, broad-billed birds renowned for their fishing expertise.

BELTED KINGFISHER
Ceryle alcyon

Size: 10-14 in. (25-36 cm)
Description: Stocky, crested blue-gray bird with a large head and bill.
Habitat: Near wooded ponds, lakes and rivers.
Comments: Often seen perched over clear water. Hovers over water before plunging in headfirst after fish. Has a loud, rattling call.

WOODPECKERS

These strong-billed birds are usually spotted on tree trunks chipping away bark in search of insects.

NORTHERN FLICKER
Colaptes auratus

Size: 10-13 in. (25-33 cm)
Description: Brownish woodpecker with a spotted breast and black bib. Underwing and undertail feathers are either red or yellow. Males have a 'mustache' that is either red or black.
Habitat: Rural and urban woodlands.
Comments: White rump patch is conspicuous in flight.

DOWNY WOODPECKER
Picoides pubescens

Size: 5-7 in. (13-18 cm)
Description: A small, sparrow-sized, black and white woodpecker with a small bill. Males have a red head patch.
Habitat: Wooded areas.
Comments: Occurs in the same habitat as the similar, larger, hairy woodpecker (*Picoides villosus*).

THREE-TOED WOODPECKER
Picoides tridactylus

Size: 7-9 in. (18-23 cm)
Description: Dark woodpecker has a black and white barred stripe on its back and sides. Males have yellow forehead patch.
Habitat: Spruce forests.
Comments: Alaska's most common and widespread woodpecker.

FLYCATCHERS

These compact birds characteristically sit on exposed perches and dart out to capture passing insects.

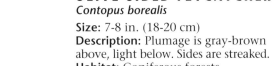

OLIVE-SIDED FLYCATCHER
Contopus borealis

Size: 7-8 in. (18-20 cm)
Description: Plumage is gray-brown above, light below. Sides are streaked.
Habitat: Coniferous forests.
Comments: Energetic song – *whip three beers* – is often heard along forest edges. One of several flycatchers found in Alaska.

LARKS

Terrestrial, slender-billed birds found in fields with low vegetation.

HORNED LARK
Eremophila alpestris

Size: 7-8 in. (18-20 cm)
Description: Brown bird with a yellow face, dark neck and eye marks and black 'horns.'
Habitat: Tundra, coastal areas during migration.
Comments: Nests and feeds on the ground. Often found in flocks.

SWALLOWS

These acrobatic fliers have short bills, long pointed wings and long tails (often forked). Their wide mouths are adapted for scooping up insects on the wing. Six species are found in Alaska.

TREE SWALLOW
Tachycineta bicolor

Size: 5-7 in. (13-18 cm)
Description: Plumage is glossy blue-black above, white below. Dark hood encloses eye.
Habitat: Open and semi-wooded areas near water in summer.
Comments: The somewhat similar bank swallow (*Riparia riparia*), is brown above and white below with a brown necklace.

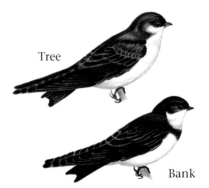

Tree

Bank

BARN SWALLOW
Hirundo rustica

Size: 6-7 in. (15-18 cm)
Description: Blue-black above, cinnamon below, it is easily identified in flight by its long, forked tail.
Habitat: Common near towns in the southeast.
Comments: Typically nests in building eaves and under bridges.

JAYS AND ALLIES

These medium to large birds are omnivorous and feed on a wide variety of plant and animal matter.

STELLER'S JAY
Cyanocitta stelleri

Size: 12-14 in. (30-36 cm)
Description: Prominent crest is key field mark. Head and shoulders are brown-black; wings, tail and belly are deep blue.
Habitat: Coniferous forests in southeast and southcentral Alaska.
Comments: Very gregarious, it frequents campsites and human dwellings in search of handouts.

COMMON RAVEN
Corvus corax

Size: 22-27 in. (56-69 cm)
Description: A large black bird with a heavy bill, wedge-shaped tail and shaggy head and throat feathers.
Habitat: Variable.
Comments: Distinguished from crows by its large size and low, croaking call. Despite its call, it is classified as a songbird.

GRAY JAY
Perisoreus canadensis

Size: 10-14 in. (25-36 cm)
Description: Puffy gray bird with a white forehead and a dark cap.
Habitat: Forests throughout Alaska.
Comments: Bold and gregarious, it is easily attracted to feeders.

BLACK-BILLED MAGPIE
Pica pica

Size: 18-22 in. (46-56 cm)
Description: Beautifully marked black-and-white bird with a long tail.
Habitat: Thickets, open areas.
Comments: Often spotted along roadways. Feeds on berries, fruit, small animals and carrion.

CHICKADEES
These small, puffy birds are very active and inquisitive.

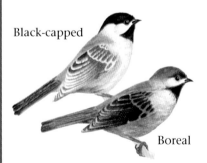

Black-capped

Boreal

BLACK-CAPPED CHICKADEE
Parus atricapillus

BOREAL CHICKADEE
Parus hudsonicus

Size: 4-6 in. (10-15 cm)
Description: Distinguished by their fluffy plumage. The black-capped chickadee has a black cap and bib. The boreal chickadee has a brown cap and a black bib.
Habitat: Forests.
Comments: The chestnut-backed chickadee (*P. rufescens*) found in southern Alaska has a black cap and bib and a red-brown back.

DIPPERS

Plump, stubby-tailed birds feed in fast-flowing streams.

AMERICAN DIPPER
Cinclus mexicanus

Size: 7-8 in. (18-20 cm)
Description: Charcoal gray bird with short tail.
Habitat: Near running water.
Comments: Found throughout Alaska, it dives, swims, and even walks along stream bottoms while feeding on invertebrates and small fishes.

NUTHATCHES

Nuthatches are stout little birds with thin, sharp bills and stumpy tails.

RED-BREASTED NUTHATCH
Sitta canadensis

Size: 5-6 in. (13-15 cm)
Description: Chunky, white-faced, grayish bird with black cap and eye line, rusty underparts and short, sharp bill.
Habitat: Forests.
Comments: Creeps about on tree trunks and branches searching for insects, often descending head first.

KINGLETS

Tiny active woodland birds.

GOLDEN-CROWNED KINGLET
Regulus satrapa

Size: 3-4 in. (8-10 cm)
Description: Small brown-gray bird has black cap with a yellowish patch in the center.
Habitat: Forests.
Comments: Often flicks wings nervously when hopping about. One of the most common birds in southeast Alaska.

THRUSHES

This group of woodland birds includes many good singers. Sexes are similar in most.

AMERICAN ROBIN
Turdus migratorius

Size: 9-11 in. (23-28 cm)
Description: Gray bird with rusty breast is familiar to most.
Habitat: Variable, from cities to arctic tundra.
Comments: Song is a rising and falling – *cheer-up, cheerily, cheer-up.*

VARIED THRUSH
Ixoreus naevius

Size: 9-11 in. (22-27 cm)
Description: Dark above and orange below, it has an orange line behind its eye and two orange wing bars.
Habitat: Primarily coniferous forests.
Comments: Forages on the ground for insects, invertebrates and seeds.

WAXWINGS

These gregarious birds are named for their red wing marks which look like waxy droplets.

BOHEMIAN WAXWING
Bombycilla garrulus

Size: 6-8 in. (15-20 cm)
Description: Distinguished by its sleek, crested head, red wing marks and red undertail coverts.
Habitat: Muskegs, forests.
Comments: Diet consists largely of berries and insects. In fall and winter, large flocks frequent urban areas where they feed on the berries of trees and shrubs.

WARBLERS AND ALLIES

Members of this large family are distinguished from other small birds by their thin, pointed bills.

YELLOW WARBLER
Dendroica petechia

Size: 4-5 in. (10-13 cm)
Description: Distinctive yellow bird with a streaked breast.
Habitat: Shrub thickets, mixed woodlands.
Comments: Song is a cheery *sweet, sweet, sweet*. The yellow Wilson's warbler (*Wilsonia pusilla*) has a black cap.

YELLOW-RUMPED WARBLER
Dendroica coronata

Size: 5-6 in. (13-15 cm)
Description: Gray-black bird has yellow rump and yellow patch before each wing. Spring males have yellow caps and a white or yellow throat. Females are brownish with similar yellow markings.
Habitat: Coniferous and mixed forests, thickets.
Comments: Formerly two species, the 'myrtle' and 'Audubon's' warblers. Abundant in spring, they feed on insects and berries.

Myrtle form

Audubon's form

ORANGE-CROWNED WARBLER
Vermivora celata

Size: 4-5 in. (10-13 cm)
Description: Drab olive bird with yellowish underparts and an orange crown patch.
Habitat: Open woodland, brushy areas.
Comments: Crown patch is often concealed. Song is a rising or falling trill.

FINCHES, SPARROWS AND ALLIES

Members of this family have short, thick, seed-cracking bills.

COMMON REDPOLL
Carduelis flammea

Size: 5-6 in. (13-15 cm)
Description: Small brownish bird with a red forehead and black chin. Male has rosy breast in winter.
Habitat: Tundra in summer; brushy areas in winter.
Comments: The similar hoary redpoll (*C. hornemanni*) is more whitish overall and the male lacks a rosy breast. Both are common at feeders.

LAPLAND LONGSPUR
Calcarius lappoinicus

Size: 5-6 in. (13-15 cm)
Description: Breeding male has a black crown, face and neck and a red-brown nape. Female has a pale, red-brown nape and a black-flecked neck.
Habitat: Tundra in summer; open areas (beaches etc.) in winter.
Comments: Feeds on the ground on seeds and insects.

SNOW BUNTING
Plectrophenax nivalis

Size: 6-8 in. (16-20 cm)
Description: Grayish-white and black summer male is unmistakable. Female is similar. Both sexes are brown in winter with white bellies.
Habitat: Tundra and coast in summer; open areas in winter.
Comments: Is often observed 'bathing' in the snow during winter. Frequents towns and camps and is called the 'house sparrow of the north.'

SAVANNAH SPARROW
Passerculus sandwichensis

Size: 5-6 in. (13-15 cm)
Description: Distinguished by its heavily, streaked plumage and light – often yellowish – stripe above each eye.
Habitat: Tundra, beaches and meadows in summer.
Comments: The most common sparrow in Alaska, it is found throughout the state in summer. The fox sparrow (*Passerella iliaca*) has a gray-brown back and a reddish tail and rump.

PINE GROSBEAK
Pinicola enucleator

Size: 8-10 in. (20-25 cm)
Description: Large, finch-like bird with a black, conical bill. Male is rosy red with black wings. Female is gray with a greenish head and rump.
Habitat: Forests, urban areas in winter.
Comments: A resident species common at feeders throughout the year.

DARK-EYED JUNCO
Junco hyemalis

Size: 5-7 in. (13-18 cm)
Description: Key field marks are dark head, pale bill, light belly and white-edged tail. 'Slate-colored' form has gray sides and a gray back; 'Oregon' form has a black head and a brown back.
Habitat: Coniferous forests and mixed woods, muskegs.
Comments: Gregarious and easily attracted to feeders. There are a total of five 'forms' of this species that vary geographically.

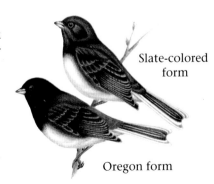

Slate-colored form

Oregon form

WHAT ARE REPTILES AND AMPHIBIANS?

Reptiles and amphibians represent a diverse array of water- and land-dwelling animals. Unfortunately, few of these temperature-sensitive, cold-blooded creatures are able to tolerate Alaska's climate.

REPTILES

Reptiles can generally be described as scaly-skinned, terrestrial creatures that breathe through lungs. The majority reproduce by laying eggs on land; in some, the eggs develop inside the mother who later gives birth to live young. Contrary to popular belief, very few are harmful to man. All are valuable in controlling rodent and insect populations.

The most common types of North American reptiles are turtles, lizards and snakes. The only reptiles found in or near Alaska are two species of marine turtle and a garter snake that are rarely encountered.

AMPHIBIANS

Amphibians are smooth-skinned, limbed vertebrates that live in moist habitats and breathe through either lungs, skin, gills, or a combination of all three. While they spend much of their lives on land, they still depend on a watery environment to complete their life cycle. Most reproduce by laying eggs in or near water. The young hatch as swimming larvae – tadpoles, for example – which breathe through gills. After a short developmental period, the larvae metamorphose into young adults with lungs and legs.

The most common types of North American amphibians are salamanders, frogs and toads. Of the seven species of amphibians found Alaska, only two are common.

HOW TO IDENTIFY FROGS AND TOADS

Frogs and toads are easy to locate since they announce their presence loudly during breeding season. Frogs are typically found in wet areas on or near the water. Toads are usually more terrestrial and may be found far from water, especially during the day.

FROGS AND TOADS

Frogs and toads are squat amphibians common near ponds and lakes. All have large heads, large eyes, long hind legs and long, sticky tongues which they use to catch insects. Most have well-developed ears and strong voices. Only males are vocal.

Toads can be distinguished from frogs by their dry, warty skin and prominent glands behind their eyes (parotoids). Some also have swellings between their eyes (bosses). When handled roughly by would-be predators, the warts and glands secrete a poisonous substance which makes the toads extremely unpalatable. Contrary to popular belief, handling toads does not cause warts.

WOOD FROG
Rana sylvatica

Size: 1-3 in. (3-8 cm)
Description: Pink to red-brown frog has a dark mask ending behind the ear, a white stripe along the upper jaw and prominent ridges along its back. Underside is uniformly light-colored.
Habitat: Damp woodlands, open areas, tundra.
Comments: Alaska's most widely distributed amphibian, it is found throughout most of the state and as far north as the Brooks Range. Staccato call is duck-like. It is usually active during daylight hours to take advantage of the sun's heat.

BOREAL TOAD
Bufo boreas

Size: 3-4 in. (8-10 cm)
Description: Large green-brown to gray toad has warts surrounded by dark blotches and a light dorsal stripe. Has oval parotoid gland behind its eye.
Habitat: Open areas near water in the southeast.
Comments: They are often seen walking, rather than hopping, in the open. Males have a soft, clucking call.

WHAT ARE FISHES?

Fishes are cold-blooded vertebrates that live in water and breathe dissolved oxygen through organs called gills. They are generally characterized by their size, shape, feeding habits, and water temperature preference. Most live in either saltwater or freshwater, though a few species divide their lives between the two (these are referred to as anadromous fishes).

All fishes have streamlined bodies covered in scales, and swim by flexing their bodies from side to side. Their fins help to steer while swimming and can also act as brakes. Many species possess an internal air bladder which acts as a depth regulator. By secreting gases into the bladder or absorbing gases from it, they are able to control the depth at which they swim.

Most fish reproduce by laying eggs freely in the water. In many, the male discharges sperm over the eggs as they are laid by the female. Depending on the species, eggs may float, sink, become attached to vegetation, or be buried.

HOW TO IDENTIFY FISHES

First, note the size, shape and color of the fish. Are there any distinguishing field marks like the double dorsal fins of rockfishes or the downturned lips of suckers? Is the body thin or torpedo-shaped? Note the orientation and placement of fins on the body. Consult the text to confirm identification.

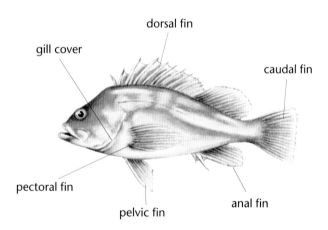

LAMPREYS

Lampreys are members of the most primitive order of fishes.

PACIFIC LAMPREY
Lampetra tridentata

Size: To 30 in. (76 cm)
Description: Identified by its slender
eel-like body, round gill openings
and sucker-like mouth.
Habitat: Anadromous.
Comments: Feeds by attaching
itself to a host fish and sucking
out fluids.

SHARKS AND ALLIES

These fishes lack bones and have skeletons completely composed of
cartilage. They lack an internal air bladder and must swim continuously
or sink to the bottom.

SPINY DOGFISH
Squalus acanthias

Size: To 5 ft. (1.5 m)
Description: Gray-brown shark has a
spine at the front of each dorsal fin.
Sides often covered with light spots.
Habitat: Shallow water to
depths of 120 ft. (36 m).
Comments: Very common
in southern coastal waters
and considered a pest by anglers.

HERRINGS AND ALLIES

Found in large schools, they are important forage and bait fishes.

PACIFIC HERRING
Clupea pallasii

Size: To 18 in. (46 cm)
Description: Greenish above,
silvery below, with a short
dorsal fin and a deeply-forked
tail.
Habitat: Inshore waters.
Comments: Quantities of sticky eggs
deposited on kelp and rocks during
spawning are widely harvested for
overseas markets.

TROUT, SALMON AND ALLIES

This diverse group includes many popular sport fishes. Most have robust bodies, square caudal fins, an adipose fin and strong teeth. Trout are found primarily in fresh water; salmon are anadromous and live in salt-water for one or more years before returning to freshwater to spawn.

SHEEFISH
Stenodus leucicthys

Size: To 4 ft. (1.2 m)
Description: Large silvery fish with a jutting lower jaw.
Habitat: Waterways in northern and western Alaska.
Comments: Renowned for its fighting ability, some call it 'Eskimo tarpon.' Is the largest of several species of silvery whitefish found in Alaska. All are important subsistence foods for native people.

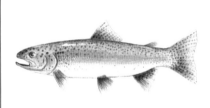

RAINBOW TROUT
Oncorhynchus mykiss

Size: To 45 in. (1.1 m)
Description: A dark-spotted fish named for the distinctive reddish band running down its side. Band is most prominent during spring spawning.
Habitat: Abundant in cold streams, reservoirs and lakes.
Comments: Both freshwater and anadromous races occur in Alaska. The sea-run version of this species (called 'steelhead') is silvery with black spots on its sides and most fins.

ARCTIC CHAR
Salvelinus alpinus

Size: To 39 in. (1 m)
Description: Color is variable, ranging from red and brown to green. Side spots are pink to red.
Habitat: Anadromous.
Comments: An important subsistence fish for native people, they were traditionally harvested using stone weirs (dam-like traps) and spears.

LAKE TROUT
Salvelinus namaycush

Size: To 4 ft. (1.2 m)
Description: A blue to greenish fish with numerous light spots on its head, body and dorsal and caudal fins. Note deeply forked tail.
Habitat: Deep lakes and waterways.
Comments: The largest trout in North America, the state record catch weighed 47 lbs. (21.3 kg).

DOLLY VARDEN
Salvelinus malma

Size: To 25 in. (64 cm)
Description: Color is variable from olive-brown to dark blue above. Spots may be brown or red-orange.
Habitat: Coastal waters.
Comments: Like salmon, it spawns in freshwater and spends much of its adult life in saltwater. Unlike salmon, it often winters in freshwater lakes and streams.

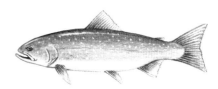

ARCTIC GRAYLING
Thymallus arcticus

Size: To 30 in. (76 cm)
Description: Distinguished at a glance by its huge purple to black dorsal fin. Caudal fin is forked.
Habitat: Clear streams and lakes.
Comments: An esteemed sport fish, it is found throughout most of mainland Alaska.

COHO SALMON
Oncorhynchus kisutch

Size: To 39 in. (1 m)
Description: Back and upper lobe of caudal fin are black-spotted. Breeding male is green-blue above and white below with brick red sides. At sea, color is silvery.
Habitat: Anadromous.
Comments: Also called silver salmon, they spend 2-3 years at sea before returning to spawn.

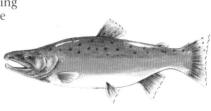

FISHES

SOCKEYE SALMON
Oncorhynchus nerka

Size: To 33 in. (84 cm)
Description: Blue-green above, and silvery below, it lacks dark spots on its back or fins. Spawning male has bright red body, green head, humped back and hooked jaw.
Habitat: Anadromous.
Comments: Sockeye support one of the state's most important commercial fisheries. Populations of sockeye that become landlocked in freshwater are called 'kokanee.'

CHUM SALMON
Oncorhynchus keta

Size: To 39 in. (1 m)
Description: This salmon lacks black spots and has white-edged lower fins. Spawning male has blotchy red sides.
Habitat: Anadromous.
Comments: Also called dog salmon. Large quantities of chum are dried by native people in summer and serve as an important year-round food source. It spawns in streams close to the ocean in late fall and winter.

PINK SALMON
Oncorhynchus gorbuscha

Size: To 30 in. (76 cm)
Description: Silvery blue-green fish has large oval spots on both lobes of its tail fin. Breeding male develops a humped back and pinkish side stripes.
Habitat: Anadromous.
Comments: Also called humpback salmon or humpies. The smallest salmon, they spend the least time at sea and return to spawn about every two years.

CHINOOK SALMON
Oncorhynchus tshawytscha

Size: To 58 in. (1.6 m)
Description: Blue to green above,
it has irregular black spots on its
back and caudal fin. Gums are
black at base of teeth.
Habitat: Anadromous.
Comments: The largest salmon,
it can weigh over 100 lbs. (45 kg).
Typically enters freshwater and
spawns in summer with some travelling over 1,000 miles (1,600 km) to
spawn in the Yukon Territory. Also
called king salmon.

Alaska's State Fish

SMELTS

Family of slender, silvery fishes that are abundant in fresh- and saltwater.

EULACHON
Thaleichtys pacificus

Size: To 11 in. (28 cm)
Description: Bluish to brown above
with dark speckling along its back.
Note large mouth.
Habitat: Anadromous.
Comments: Also called candlefish,
it is so oily it can be fitted with a
wick and burned once dried. The
similar capelin (*Mallotus villosus*),
spawns in large numbers in nearshore waters.

MUDMINNOWS

Mudminnows are able to survive extreme cold and stagnant water. They are
one of few fish in the world that are able to breathe air both in and out of
the water.

ALASKA BLACKFISH
Dallia pectoralis

Size: To 13 in. (33 cm)
Description: Elongate, cylindrical
fish has dark, blotchy skin. Note
rounded tail.
Habitat: Freshwater lakes and
rivers in northern half of Alaska.
Comments: An important subsistence fish for native people, it is
caught throughout the autumn
and winter.

PIKE

Large, predatory fishes are easily distinguished by their duck-like snout.

NORTHERN PIKE
Esox lucius

Size: To 53 in. (1.3 m)
Description: Elongate fish is olive to green brown above and light below. Sides are covered with bean-shaped spots.
Habitat: Streams, rivers and lakes with abundant vegetation.
Comments: Voracious predator that feeds primarily on fish but will eat any animal it can swallow.

SUCKERS

Suckers have distinctive, downturned fleshy lips that they use to 'vacuum' the bottom of lakes and streams in search of invertebrates.

LONGNOSE SUCKER
Catostomus catostomus

Size: To 24 in. (60 cm)
Description: Elongate, cylindrical fish with a bulbous snout projecting far beyond its lips. Sides are olive to blue and belly is white.
Habitat: Deep, clear lakes and streams.
Comments: Unlike many bottom-feeding fishes, suckers lack mouth barbels.

CODS & ALLIES

All have long tapering bodies and long dorsal and anal fins. Barbels are often present.

BURBOT
Lota lota

Size: To 3 ft. (90 cm)
Description: Elongate brown to greenish fish with a large head and a single chin whisker. Black mottling occurs on sides and back.
Habitat: Deep lakes and rivers.
Comments: The only true freshwater cod, they are widespread throughout most of Alaska. Spawns in winter under the ice.

WALLEYE POLLOCK
Theragra chalcogramma

Size: To 3 ft. (90 cm)
Description: This elongate, greenish fish has 3 dorsal fins and 2 anal fins. Lower jaw projects slightly. Sides are silvery.
Habitat: Open sea from surface to depths of 1,200 ft. (366 m).
Comments: An important commercial species, it is especially abundant in the Bering Sea where millions are harvested annually.

STICKLEBACKS

These small fishes are named for the defined row of spines along their back. Noted for their mating behavior, the males are responsible for building intricate, suspended nests and guarding their eggs and young.

NINESPINE STICKLEBACK
Pungitius pungitius

Size: To 4 in. (10 cm)
Description: Slender greenish fish distinguished by the row of (usually) nine short spines ahead of the dorsal fin.
Habitat: Found in shallow, vegetated streams, pools and small lakes.
Comments: Diet consists of crustaceans, insects and algae. The three-spine stickleback (*Gasterosteus aculeatus*) is locally common in southern and western Alaska.

ROCKFISH

Most members of this large family have prominent, spiky dorsal fins and large eyes. Following are two of the several species found in Alaskan waters.

YELLOWEYE ROCKFISH
Sebastes ruberrimus

Size: To 36 in. (91 cm)
Description: Reddish to orange fish with large, bright yellow eyes with black-edged fins. Depending on age, it has one or two light side stripes.
Habitat: Shallow to deep rocky reefs.
Comments: Often called red snapper by Alaskans, it is long-lived and may reach over 100 years of age.

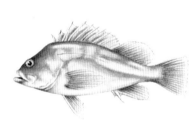

COPPER ROCKFISH
Sebastes caurinus

Size: To 22 in. (56 cm)
Description: Brown-olive to red-brown fish with light patches on its sides. Often has a prominent light stripe extending from mid-body to the tail.
Habitat: Nearshore water to depths of 600 ft. (182 m).
Comments: Like most rockfish, it has venomous spines near its dorsal, anal and pelvic fins and should be handled with care to avoid injury.

GREENLINGS

Fishes with long bodies and long dorsal and anal fins.

LINGCOD
Ophiodon elongatus

Size: To 5 ft. (1.5 m)
Description: Large green-brown fish with a jutting lower jaw and a long, spiny, notched dorsal fin.
Habitat: Rocky bottoms in nearshore waters.
Comments: An important sport and commercial fish, they are voracious predators.

KELP GREENLING
Hexagrammus decagrammus
Size: To 20 in. (50 cm)
Description: Dark males are easily distinguished by their bright blue spots.
Habitat: Kelp beds, nearshore areas.
Comments: Feeds primarily on small crustaceans and is an important forage species for Alaskan game fish.

SCULPINS

This family of over 300 species are common in fresh- and saltwater and are the common small fishes found in intertidal areas.

SLIMY SCULPIN
Cottus cognatus
Size: To 4 in. (10 cm)
Description: Small, dark, mottled fish has a large head and bulging eyes.
Habitat: Cold, clear streams.
Comments: It and the related coastrange sculpin (*C. aleuticus*) are found throughout Alaska.

FLATFISHES

Flattened fishes have both eyes on the same side of the body. They often lie on the bottom buried in sediment with only their eyes exposed.

PACIFIC HALIBUT
Hippoglossus stenolepis
Size: To 9 ft. (2.7 m)
Description: Flat, diamond-shaped fish is mottled brown above and whitish below. Note long dorsal fin.
Habitat: Widely distributed along bottom to edge of continental shelf.
Comments: Supports one of Alaska's most valuable fisheries. A highly esteemed food and sport fish, the state record catch weighed 495 lbs. (224 kg).

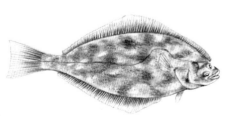

WHAT IS SEASHORE LIFE?

This section includes a variety of animal and plant groups. Most species can be readily observed in tidal pools or shallow waters. All of the animals in this section are classed as invertebrates or 'animals without backbones.'

The best time to observe the greatest variety of species is during low tide. Tide times are often published in newspapers, and tide tables are available at most sporting goods stores. There are generally two tides a day, and tidal differences are typically as much as 15 ft. (4.5 m).* The lowest tides of the year occur in midwinter and midsummer.

The main groups covered in this section include marine plants, coelenterates, sea stars and allies, crustaceans and mollusks.

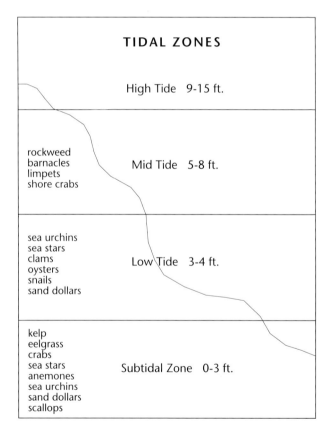

TIDAL ZONES

High Tide   9-15 ft.

rockweed
barnacles
limpets
shore crabs

Mid Tide   5-8 ft.

sea urchins
sea stars
clams
oysters
snails
sand dollars

Low Tide   3-4 ft.

kelp
eelgrass
crabs
sea stars
anemones
sea urchins
sand dollars
scallops

Subtidal Zone   0-3 ft.

* The Cook Inlet near Anchorage has the second greatest tide range in North America with spring tides fluctuating nearly 40 ft. (12 m).

MARINE PLANTS

This general group includes a few of the most common coastal marine plants.

BULL KELP
Nereocystis luetkeana

Size: To 100 ft. long (30 m)
Description: A number of long brownish blades radiate from a single float at the water's surface. Long, tubular stem is anchored to the bottom by a 'holdfast.'
Habitat: Found in dense beds along shorelines.
Comments: Kelp beds provide an important source of food and cover for invertebrates, fishes, birds and marine mammals.

ROCKWEED
Fucus distichus

Size: To 20 in. (50 cm)
Description: A ragged, brownish plant with swollen air bladders along a ribbed stem.
Habitat: Rocky shorelines.
Comments: Also called bladder wrack, it is found worldwide. Parts of plants torn off by waves often become reestablished as new plants.

EELGRASS
Zostera marina

Size: Blades to 5 ft. (1.5 m)
Description: Tall slender plant with grass-like leaves.
Habitat: Muddy and sandy soils.
Comments: Eelgrass serves as an important nursery habitat for many kinds of fishes and invertebrates.

SURFGRASS
Phllospadix spp.

Size: Blades to 6 ft. (2 cm)
Description: Bright emerald-green leaves grow in dense clumps.
Habitat: Tidepools and exposed rocky shores.
Comments: Several similar species of surfgrass grow along the coast.

SEA SACK
Halosaccion glandiforme

Size: To 6 in. (15 cm)
Description: Small weiner-shaped bulbs grow in clumps. Color ranges from yellowish to purple.
Habitat: Mid-tide zone.
Comments: Each sac is filled with gas produced by photosynthesis.

SEA LETTUCE
Ulva lactuca

Size: To 20 in. (51 cm)
Description: Bright green, lettuce-like algae blade.
Habitat: Attached to rocks exposed to moderate waves.
Comments: An edible algae that is high in vitamins, it is eaten by many cultures around the world.

COELENTERATES

This group contains a variety of free-swimming and colonial creatures including jellyfish, hydroids, anemones and corals.

GIANT GREEN ANEMONE
Anthopleura xanthogrammica

Size: To 10 in. wide (25 cm)
Description: Flattened, green disk with numerous, uniform tentacles.
Habitat: Common in tide pools on exposed shores.
Comments: Algae living in the tissues of the animal are responsible for its color.

BROODING ANEMONE
Epiactis prolifera

Size: To 2 in. wide (5 cm)
Description: Flower-like anemone may be pink, red, blue, brown or orange.
Habitat: Unprotected coasts from the high tide line to 25 ft. (7.6 m) depths.
Comments: Broods young near base of column.

AGGREGATE ANEMONE
Anthopleura elegantissima

Size: To 15 in. tall (40 cm)
Description: Column is green to white. Pale tentacles have blue, pink or purple tips.
Habitat: Attached to rocks, pilings in shallow waters.
Comments: Like all anemones, it uses its stinging tentacles to subdue prey before engulfing it.

FRILLED ANEMONE
Metridium senile

Size: To 3 ft. tall (90 cm)
Description: Tall brown, yellow or white anemone has abundant slender tentacles.
Habitat: Nearshore waters.
Comments: Often grows attached to wharf pilings and other submerged solid objects.

MOON JELLYFISH
Aurelia aurita

Size: To 16 in. wide (40 cm)
Description: Told by white, translucent, bell-shaped body with fringe
of stinging tentacles.
Habitat: Surface of the ocean.
Comments: Commonly washes
ashore following storms. Be wary of
handling since its stinging tentacles
can cause an itchy rash.

LION'S MANE JELLYFISH
Cyanea capillata

Size: To 8 ft. wide (2.4 m)
Description: Large, bell-shaped,
yellowish jellyfish has a shaggy
'mane' of hanging, stinging tentacles.
Habitat: Surface of the ocean.
Comments: Feared by fishermen
when it fouls their gear, its highly
toxic venom causes burning and blis-
tering.

SEA STARS AND ALLIES

These mostly bottom-dwelling animals are characterized by spiny
bodies and radial symmetry, i.e., body parts repeat around a central
hub, as in a wheel. The 'arms' are usually arranged in multiples of 5,
and may be short or long, cylindrical or flattened.

OCHRE SEA STAR
Pisaster ochraceus

Size: To 14 in. (35 cm)
Description: Identified by its short
rays and patterned surface. Body
color may be purple, yellow, orange
or brown.
Habitat: Common in tidepools and
attached to rocks at low tide.
Comments: Like most sea stars, it is
capable of regenerating severed
body parts. Sea stars, once called
starfish, are not closely related to
fish.

GIANT SPINED SEA STAR
Pisaster giganteus

Size: To 2 ft. (60 cm)
Description: Large sea star may be red, brown, tan or purple. Delicate spines have blue rings around their base.
Habitat: Found on rocks during low tides.
Comments: Although sea stars have no jaws, most are carnivorous and very destructive to shellfish populations.

DAISY BRITTLE STAR
Opiopholis aculeata

Size: To 8 in. wide (20 cm)
Description: Five, slender rays radiate from scalloped central disk. May be red, pink, white, blue, green or tan colored.
Habitat: Tidepools to deep ocean waters.
Comments: Common under rocks and in crevices.

BAT STAR
Patria miniata

Size: To 10 in. (25 cm)
Description: Robust, short-armed sea star. Color ranges from white to red.
Habitat: Rocky and sandy areas from tidepools to deep ocean waters.
Comments: Also called the sea bat.

SAND DOLLAR
Dendraster excentricus

Size: To 4 in. (10 cm)
Description: Flattened brown animal is covered with short spines. Upper surface of shell has a 5-petal design.
Habitat: Found at low tides on sandy beaches, often partially buried.
Comments: Skeletons of sand dollars (tests) are bleached white and retain the flower-like impression.

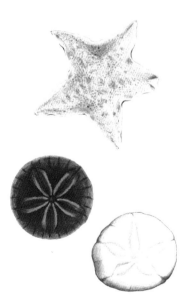

Skeleton

PURPLE SEA URCHIN
Strongylocentrotus purpuratus

Size: 4 in. (10 cm)
Description: Told at a glance by its red-purple color, rounded body and long spines.
Habitat: Rocky shores at and below the low tide line, it is especially common on open coastlines.
Comments: Is commercially harvested for its gonads which are sold as a sushi delicacy in Japan.

GREEN SEA URCHIN
Strongylocentrotus droebachiensis

Size: 3 in. (8 cm)
Description: Green oval creature with long pointed spines.
Habitat: Rocky shores near the low tide line.
Comments: Feeds primarily on algae. Empty skeletons of sea urchins (tests) often wash up on beaches.

Urchin Test

CRUSTACEANS

Most crustaceans live near saltwater and have a hard external skeleton, antennae and paired limbs. The limbs differ greatly in form and function, and are modified for specific purposes in different species.

PURPLE SHORE CRAB
Hemigrapsus nudas

Size: To 2 in. (5 cm)
Description: Distinguished by its deep purple body and red-spotted claws. Red-brown, green and yellow variants also exist.
Habitat: Open rocky shores.
Comments: Often found scuttling about on intertidal rocks.

ALASKAN KING CRAB
Paralithodes camtschatica

Size: To 5 ft. (1.5 m)
Description: Huge red crab with
a spiked shell has four visible pair
of legs. The right pincer claw is
usually larger on adults.
Habitat: Intertidal waters to
depths of 200 ft. (61 m).
Comments: Since statehood,
king crabs have been Alaska's
second most valuable
commercial species next
to sockeye salmon. Two
other similar species found
here include the blue and golden
king crabs (*P. platypus* and *Lithodes
aequispina* respectively).

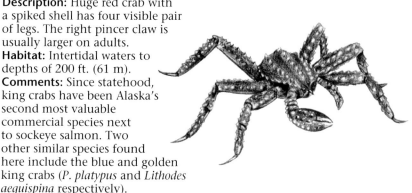

DUNGENESS CRAB
Cancer magister

Size: To 12 in. (30 cm)
Description: Large red-brown crab.
Sexes can be distinguished by the
shape of their abdomens; male's is V-
shaped, female's is U-shaped.
Habitat: Young are found in sandy
pools near low-tide line; older
individuals gradually migrate to
deeper waters.
Comments: This crab is often sold in
markets.

RED CRAB
Cancer productus

Size: To 7 in. (18 cm)
Description: Distinguished by fan-
shaped shell and brick-red color.
Habitat: Rocky shores, estuaries.
Comments: Young crabs are highly
variable in color and often have
streaked shells.

HERMIT CRAB
Pagurus spp.

Size: 1-2 in. (3-5 cm)
Description: Small crab lives in discarded snail shell. Has two pair of walking legs.
Habitat: Common intertidally in tide pools or on mud or sand.
Comments: Several similar-looking species of hermit crabs are found along Alaskan shores.

SHRIMP
Pandalus spp.

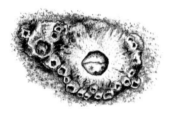

Size: To 8 in. (20 cm)
Description: Slender crustacean has a large head and several pairs of jointed legs and long antennae. Tail has two lobes. Color ranges from pink to brown.
Habitat: Variable, many in nearshore waters to depths of 200 ft. (61 m).
Comments: Five species of similar shrimp that differ mostly in size are found in Alaskan waters.

ACORN BARNACLE
Balanus glandula

Size: To 1 in. (2.5 cm)
Description: Volcano-like gray shell often grows in clusters attached to rocks and piers at the high tide line.
Habitat: Coastal.
Comments: Barnacles hatch as free-swimming larvae which eventually attach themselves to solid objects and mature into shelled adults. They feed by opening plates at the top of their shells and extending feathery arms to trap small organisms.

GOOSENECK BARNACLE
Lepas anatifera

Size: To 2 in. (5 cm)
Description: Flexible stalk topped with 5 hard whitish plates.
Habitat: Widely distributed in open coastal waters.
Comments: Clusters are often found attached to floating objects.

MOLLUSKS

This large group of soft-bodied and usually hard-shelled invertebrates occupies many habitats in water and on land. The mouth of most mollusks – excluding bivalves – has a ribbon-like toothed structure called a radula which helps the animals break down food or capture prey.

ROUGH KEYHOLE LIMPET
Diodera aspera

Size: To 2 in. (5 cm)
Description: Cone-shaped shell has side ribs and a hole in the top.
Habitat: Found intertidally on kelp and rocks.
Comments: Color of shell ranges from white to tan and gray and is influenced by the kinds of animals that colonize the shell surface.

LINED CHITON
Tonicella lineata

Size: 2 in. (5 cm)
Description: Purplish to pink shell is made up of loosely connected plates.
Habitat: Intertidal waters to depths of 200 ft. (61 m).
Comments: If handled, it usually rolls into a ball.

ALASKAN ABALONE
Haliotis kamtschatkana

Size: 5-6 in. (13-15 cm)
Description: Large, oval shell has four to six holes along its edge. Color varies between red, white, green and blue. Interior is pearly white.
Habitat: Low tide to 40 ft. (12 m) depth.
Comments: Also called pinto abalone. Has been used by native people for food and decorative purposes for centuries. One of the smallest species of abalone.

NATIVE LITTLENECK CLAM
Protothaca staminea
Size: To 3 in. (8 cm)
Description: Rounded, white shell is ribbed with growth lines.
Habitat: Sandy and gravelly soils in the mid-tide region.
Comments: Feeds by extracting minute particles from the water passing over its gills.

PACIFIC RAZOR CLAM
Siliqua patula
Size: 3-6 in. (8-15 cm)
Description: Long, narrow shell is typically yellow-brown. Inside of shell is glossy white.
Habitat: Sandy beaches.
Comments: Harvested extensively throughout southern Alaska by commercial and sport fisheries. One of four species found in Alaska.

CALIFORNIA MUSSEL
Mytilus californianus
Size: To 10 in. (25 cm)
Description: Thick, oval-shaped, blue-black shell has prominent ridges.
Habitat: Intertidal waters, rock crevices.
Comments: Very abundant along rocky coasts.

BLUE MUSSEL
Mytilus edulis
Size: To 2 in. (5 cm)
Description: Blue-black shell is oval-shaped and relatively smooth.
Habitat: Intertidal waters.
Comments: Common on sheltered shores throughout the state. Often found attached to pilings, rocks and other solid objects.

NUTTALL'S COCKLE
Clinocardium nuttalli

Size: 2-6 in. (5-15 cm)
Description: Fan-shaped, brown shell is slightly inflated and has scalloped edges. Note dark concentric bands.
Habitat: In sand or mud.
Comments: Dark bands are formed during tidal cycles.

PACIFIC WEATHERVANE SCALLOP
Patinopecten cauimus

Size: To 8 in. (20 cm)
Description: Large fan-shaped shell is brownish and deeply ribbed.
Habitat: Nearshore waters to depths of 600 ft. (183 m).
Comments: Also called the giant Pacific scallop, it supports small local commercial fisheries.

PACIFIC PINK SCALLOP
Chlamys hastata

Size: To 3 in. (8 cm)
Description: Beautiful fan-shaped shell is often covered with colored sponges and may be white, yellow, orange, purple or pink.
Habitat: Intertidal waters.
Comments: Unlike other bivalves, scallops possess a set of eyes that are capable of detecting motion and light.

WHAT ARE TREES & SHRUBS

TREES

Trees can be broadly defined as perennial woody plants at least 16 ft. (5 m) tall with a single stem (trunk) and a well-developed crown of branches, twigs and leaves. Most are long-lived plants and range in age from 40-50 years for smaller deciduous trees to several hundred years for many of the conifers.

Common Tree Silhouettes

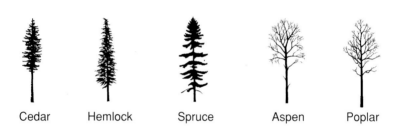

| Cedar | Hemlock | Spruce | Aspen | Poplar |

SHRUBS

Shrubs are perennial woody plants normally less than 16 ft. (5 m) tall that support a crown of branches, twigs and leaves. Unlike trees, they are anchored to the ground by several stems rather than a single trunk. Most are fast-growing and provide an important source of food and shelter for wildlife.

HOW TO IDENTIFY TREES & SHRUBS

First, note its size and shape. Does it have one or several 'trunks.' Examine the size, color, and shape of the leaves and how they are arranged on the twigs. Are they opposite or alternate? Simple or compound? Hairy or smooth? Are flowers or fruits visible on branches or on the ground? Once you've collected as much information as you can, consult the illustrations and text to confirm your sighting.

LEAF SHAPES

Elliptical   Heart-shaped   Rounded   Oval   Lobed   Lance-shaped

Leaflets

Compound Leaves

LEAF ARRANGEMENTS

Alternate   Opposite   Whorled

COMMON FRUITS

Drupe
junipers, cherries, dogwoods, hollies

Pome
apples, plums, yuccas, pears

Nut
walnuts, pecans, hickories

Berry-like
blackberries, oranges, tomatoes

Winged Seed
dandelions, milkweeds, poplars, cottonwoods

Samara
maples, ashes, hophornbeams, elms

Acorn
oaks

Pod
peas, mesquites, locusts

PINES

Most have long, needle-like leaves which grow grouped in bundles of 2-5. Male and female cones usually occur on the same tree.

SHORE PINE
Pinus contorta contorta

Size: To 75 ft. (23 m)
Description: Typically a small, shrubby tree with a domed or spired crown. Needles grow in twisted bundles of 2. Oval cones have stiff prickles at the end of each scale and grow backward along branches.
Habitat: Coastal muskegs, open areas on well drained soils.
Comments: The similar, larger lodgepole pine (*P. c. latifolia),* found in the vicinity of Skagway, has cones that grow outward along branches.

SPRUCES

Relatively large evergreens found in many habitats, they are easily distinguished by their needles that grow from woody pegs along the branches. It is much easier to roll a spruce needle between your fingers than the two-sided needles of other evergreens.

Alaska's State Tree

SITKA SPRUCE
Picea sitchensis

Size: To 230 ft. (70 m)
Description: Large tree with cylindrical crown has straight trunk, often buttressed at the base. Flattened, sharp-tipped needles grow along hairless branchlets. Elongate cones have papery scales with toothed edges.
Habitat: Moist soils from sea level to 3,300 ft. (1,000 m).
Comments: Found throughout southeast Alaska and westward to Kodiak Island, this often massive tree can live up to 800 years. It is an important food source for wildlife.

BLACK SPRUCE
Picea mariana

Size: To 30 ft. (9 m)
Description: Small to medium-sized tree has 4-sided, pale blue-green needles. Rounded purple-brown cones grow near top of tree.
Habitat: Bogs, muskegs, wet areas throughout the interior and southcentral Alaska.
Comments: Will hybridize with white and sitka spruce.

WHITE SPRUCE
Picea glauca

Size: To 75 ft. (23 m)
Description: Medium-sized tree has 4-sided, blue-green needles up to 3/4 in. (2 cm) long. Light brown, elongate cones are up to 2 in. (5 cm) long.
Habitat: Woodlands and alpine areas throughout most of Alaska.
Comments: Trees in exposed areas are often stunted. This is the most common tree in central Alaska.

HEMLOCKS

Distinguished by their thin branches and drooping crown tips. Needles are two-sided and grow singly from woody pegs along the branches.

WESTERN HEMLOCK
Tsuga heterophylla

Size: To 200 ft. (61 m)
Description: Medium to large-sized tree with a drooping crown and branches. Flat needles grow from 2 sides of twigs, parallel to the ground. Small, rounded cones (1 in./ 3 cm long) hang at ends of twigs.
Habitat: Moist, well drained soils.
Comments: The most common tree in coastal forests of southeastern and southcentral Alaska. The similar mountain hemlock (*T. mertensiana*) has elongate cones up to 2.5 in. (6 cm) long.

LARCHES

Unlike most conifers, larches are deciduous and shed their needle-like leaves in the fall. One species is found in Alaska.

TAMARACK
Larix laricina

Size: To 60 ft. (18 m)
Description: Small to medium-sized tree has a straight trunk and an irregular, open crown. Leaves grow in dense clusters of 12-24. Cones grow upright along twigs and have finely toothed scales.
Habitat: Muskegs, floodplains and wet areas in the interior.
Comments: Leaves turn yellowish in autumn before falling.

CEDARS AND ALLIES

All have scaly or awl-shaped leaves which are tightly bunched on twigs. The heavily-weighted twigs often droop at their tips

ALASKA CEDAR
Chamaecyparis nootkatensis

Size: To 100 ft. (30 m)
Description: Medium-sized evergreen with a narrow crown of drooping branches. Scale-like leaves grow along 4-sided twigs that grow in flattened, fan-shaped sprays. Small, rounded, cones have 4-6 scales with hard, pointed tips.
Habitat: Wet soils in southeast Alaska and west to Prince William Sound.
Comments: Durable, pliant wood is decay-resistant and used widely for woodworking.

COMMON JUNIPER
Juniperus communis

Size: To 10 ft. (3 m)
Description: Low, spreading shrub or small tree has an open, irregular crown. Needle-like leaves grow in whorls of 3 around twigs. Berry-like blue-black cones have 1-3 seeds.
Habitat: Rocky and sandy areas.
Comments: Widely planted as an ornamental, it is found throughout most of Alaska.

WILLOWS AND ALLIES

Most have narrow, finely-toothed leaves which grow alternately along twigs. There are 33 species in Alaska.

BEBB WILLOW
Salix bebbiana

Size: To 30 ft. (9 m)
Description: Shrub or small tree with a short trunk and a broad, rounded crown. Oblong leaves are widest at or above the middle and have prominent veins.
Habitat: Moist, open areas, borders of lakes and waterways.
Comments: Is the main source of the decorative wood called 'diamond willow' used to make furniture, canes and candleholders. The 'diamond' shapes are caused by a fungus.

FELTLEAF WILLOW
Salix alaxensis

Size: To 33 ft. (10 m)
Description: Shrub or small tree often grows prostrate in exposed sites. Leaves are usually broadest beyond the middle and covered with dense, whitish hairs. Cone-shaped fruiting capsule is covered with white hairs.
Habitat: Mixed forests, along the coast throughout Alaska.
Comments: A favorite forage of moose.

POPLARS

Found in moist habitats, these fast-growing trees are distinguished from willows by their drooping flower clusters (catkins). Alternate, unlobed leaves are toothed and generally heart-shaped.

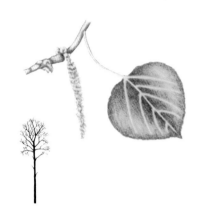

QUAKING ASPEN
Populus tremuloides

Size: To 60 ft. (18 m)
Description: Long, slender trunk supports a crown of spreading branches. Rounded leaves have long stems and the leaves rustle (tremble) in the slightest breeze. Leaves turn yellow in autumn.
Habitat: Well-drained soils in a variety of habitats.
Comments: Its twigs, leaves, catkins and bark are an important food source for wildlife.

BALSAM POPLAR
Populus balsamifera

Size: To 100 ft. (30 m)
Description: Medium to large-sized tree. Long, drooping clusters of brownish flowers bloom in spring before the leaves unfold and are succeeded by oval capsules containing numerous cottony seeds.
Habitat: Well drained soils in river valleys, forests and open areas of interior Alaska.
Comments: Capable of reproducing by seeds or from root suckers, it is a fast-growing species that quickly establishes itself in disturbed areas.

BIRCHES

Leaves are commonly oval-shaped with toothed margins. Distinctive, cylindrical, woody cones (strobiles) disintegrate in the fall when ripe.

PAPER BIRCH
Betula papyrifera

Size: To 80 ft. (24 m)
Description: Small to medium-sized tree with a straight trunk and rounded crown. Coarsely-toothed, heart-shaped leaves turn yellow in the fall. Key field mark is chalky white bark that peels off the trunk in strips. Inner bark is orange.
Habitat: Moist and sandy soils.
Comments: Often associated with spruce and poplars, it is quick to establish itself in burned-out areas. Three subspecies occur in Alaska.

ALDERS

Alders are fast-growing shrubs and trees with ragged crowns and deeply veined leaves. Woody cone persists in winter.

SITKA ALDER
Alnus sinuata

Size: To 33 ft. (10 m)
Description: Shrub or small tree with open, rounded crown. Leaves have toothed edges and are up to 6 in. (15 cm) long. Flowers mature in spring with the leaves.
Habitat: Bottomlands, disturbed areas, rocky soils.
Comments: Often forms dense thickets in wet inland areas.

GREEN ALDER
Alnus crispa

Size: To 14 ft. (4.3 m)
Description: Spreading shrub has finely toothed, sharp-pointed leaves that are shiny above, slightly hairy below. Flowers in May-June. Egg-shaped cones appear in July.
Habitat: Along waterways, forested slopes.
Comments: Alder twigs and buds are an important winter food source for the white-tailed ptarmigan.

MAPLES

Maples are distinguished by their large, opposite-growing leaves and long-winged seed pairs. The leaves are especially conspicuous in autumn when they turn vivid shades of orange, red and yellow.

DOUGLAS MAPLE
Acer glabrum

Size: To 30 ft. (9.1 m)
Description: Shrub or small tree. Leaves are up to 7 in. (18 cm) long and have reddish stalks. Greenish flowers bloom in drooping clusters in May, and are succeeded by winged seed pairs in late summer.
Habitat: Moist soils in the southeast.
Comments: The only species of maple native to Alaska, it is found along shorelines and forested slopes.

ALASKAN SHRUBS

Following are common shrubs from a variety of families. Shrubs that are most conspicuous when in bloom are included in the section on wildflowers.

NORTHERN RED CURRANT
Ribes triste

Size: To 3 ft. (91 cm)
Description: Low, spreading shrub has shredded bark. Leaves have 3-5 lobes and are up to 4 in. (10 cm) long. Red flowers bloom in drooping clusters May-June and are succeeded by red translucent berries.
Habitat: Moist woods and meadows.
Comments: One of several species of currant found in Alaska.

SALMONBERRY
Rubus spectabilis

Size: To 7 ft. (2.1 m)
Description: Often a thicket-forming shrub in south coastal Alaska. Compound leaves have 3 irregularly toothed leaflets. Showy pink to purple flowers bloom June-July and are succeeded by red, raspberry-like fruits.
Habitat: Open forests, rocky slopes.
Comments: The large, sweet berries are a favorite of bears.

CLOUDBERRY
Rubus chamaemorus

Size: To 8 in. (20 cm)
Description: Erect stems rise from a creeping rootstock. Coarse-veined, long-stemmed leaves have 5 lobes. Rounded flower with 4-5 petals blooms May-June and is succeeded by amber to yellow, raspberry-like fruits in summer.
Habitat: Bogs, muskegs and tundra throughout Alaska.
Comments: Also called baked apple-berry after the flavor of its fruit.

TRAILING RASPBERRY
Rubus pedatus

Size: To 1 in. (2.5 cm)
Description: Trailing, mat-forming vine has compound leaves with 5 lobes. White flowers have 5 narrow petals and bloom May-June. Red berries with 1-6 drupelets ripen in late summer.
Habitat: Mossy woodlands and alpine areas in southern Alaska.
Comments: The small, juicy berries are often used in preserves.

SOAPBERRY
Shepherdia canadensis

Size: To 6 ft. (1.8 m)
Description: Shrub has tiny brownish, sandpaper-like scales on young shoots and the underside of leaves. Yellowish flowers bloom in May and are succeeded by oval red berries in summer.
Habitat: Open woodlands and dry, rocky areas.
Comments: Most common in Alaska's interior.

LOW BUSH CRANBERRY
Vaccinium vitis-idaea

Size: To 8 in. (20 cm)
Description: Mat-forming shrub has shiny, oval, evergreen leaves with 'rolled' edges. Stems rise up to 8 in. (20 cm) above horizontal roots. Small, bell-shaped flowers bloom in June-July and are succeeded by bright red berries in August.
Habitat: Muskegs and alpine slopes throughout Alaska.
Comments: Berries are usually picked after the first frost and are used for jams, jellies and beverages.

HIGH BUSH CRANBERRY
Viburnum edule

Size: To 12 ft. (3.6 m)
Description: Upright shrub has opposite, rounded leaves with 3 main lobes. Leaves turn red in autumn. Small, white flowers bloom in clusters June-July and are succeeded by translucent, red or orange berries.
Habitat: Open woodlands throughout most of Alaska.
Comments: Collected extensively by Alaskans, they are often harvested after they have been 'sweetened' by the first frost of the fall.

KINNIKINNIK
Arctostaphylos uva-ursi

Size: To 3 in. (8 cm)
Description: Sprawling, mat-forming shrub has leathery, spatulate-shaped, net-veined leaves. Pinkish bell-shaped flowers bloom May-June and are succeeded by red-orange, mealy berries.
Habitat: Common in dry woods and open areas throughout Alaska.
Comments: Also called bearberry.

BOG BLUEBERRY
Vaccinium uliginosum

Size: To 16 in. (40 cm)
Description: Erect or prostrate shrub has oval, alternate leaves with smooth edges. Bell-shaped, pinkish flowers bloom in June and are succeeded by blue berries in summer.
Habitat: Muskegs, tundra and open forests throughout Alaska.
Comments: Several species of blueberry are found in Alaska including early blueberry (*V. ovalifolium*), the most common species found in southern coastal forests.

PACIFIC SERVICEBERRY
Amelanchier florida

Size: To 15 ft. (4.6 m)
Description: Shrub or small tree has oval leaves that are coarsely toothed above the middle. White, 5-petaled flowers bloom June-July and are succeeded by purplish, sweet berries.
Habitat: Open forests, rocky slopes.
Comments: Often confused with blueberries which have leaves with smooth edges.

CROWBERRY
Empetrum nigrum

Size: To 6 in. (15 cm)
Description: Mat-forming, heather-like shrub has narrow, needle-like leaves. Small maroon flowers bloom shortly after the snow melts and are succeeded by black, juicy berries.
Habitat: Muskegs and alpine slopes throughout Alaska.
Comments: Berries persist on the plant through winter and are consumed by wildlife including grouse, ptarmigan and bears.

OREGON CRABAPPLE
Malus diversifolia

Size: To 25 ft. (7.6 m)
Description: Shrub or small tree has sharply toothed elliptical leaves that are dark green above and pale below. Fragrant white flowers bloom in June and are succeeded by small, oblong 'apples.'
Habitat: Moist bottomlands in south.
Comments: Twigs and fruits are an important food source for wildlife including deer, small mammals and birds.

DEVIL'S CLUB
Oplopanax horridus

Size: To 10 ft. (3 m)
Description: Erect or sprawling shrub has leaves and stems covered with sharp spines. Large, maple-like leaves have 7-9 toothed lobes. Clusters of small, whitish flowers bloom in terminal clusters in June and are succeeded by clusters of red berries that persist into winter.
Habitat: Open forests, streambanks and ravines.
Comments: The spines readily break off and soon fester in skin if not removed. Native Alaskans believed the plant possessed magical powers and used it for various medicines and rituals.

DWARF ARCTIC BIRCH
Betula nana

Size: To 3 ft. (91 cm)
Description: Low, spreading shrub has short-stalked leaves often broader than they are long. Flowers appear in June and are succeeded by woody fruits July-August.
Habitat: Muskegs, rocky slopes, tundra.
Comments: Widespread throughout most of Alaska.

SWEETGALE
Myrica gale

Size: To 4 ft. (1.2 m)
Description: Low, spreading
shrub with elongate, coarsely
toothed leaves to 2 in. (5 cm)
long. Flowers bloom in May-June
in scaly catkins and are succeeded
by 2-winged nutlets.
Habitat: Low, wet areas.
Comments: Its flowers bloom shortly
after spring break-up and exude a
waxy scent near marshes and waterways.

RED-OSIER DOGWOOD
Cornus stolonifera

Size: To 12 ft. (3.7 m)
Description: Tall shrub has opposite
leaves with sunken veins. Clusters of
delicate white flowers bloom June-
July and are succeeded by whitish,
berry-like fruits. Dark red twigs are an
excellent winter field mark.
Habitat: Moist soils in open forest
understory and along waterways in
central and southeastern Alaska.
Comments: Plant is an important
winter browse for moose and deer.

WHAT ARE WILDFLOWERS?

Wildflowers are soft-stemmed flowering plants, usually smaller than trees or shrubs, that grow anew each year. Some regenerate annually from the same rootstock (perennials), while others grow from seeds and last a single season (annuals). Most have flowering stems bearing colorful blossoms which ripen into fruits as the growing season progresses. The flowering stem typically grows upright, but may be climbing, creeping or trailing.

The species in this section have been grouped according to color rather than family to facilitate field identification. The color groups used are:

- White
- Yellow, Orange and Green
- Red and Pink
- Blue and Purple

HOW TO IDENTIFY WILDFLOWERS

After noting color, examine the shape of the flower heads. Are they daisy-like, bell-shaped, or cross-shaped? How are they arranged on the plant? Do they occur singly or in clusters? Are the flower heads upright or drooping? Pay close attention to the leaves and how they are arranged on the stem. Refer to the illustrations and text to confirm its size, habitat and blooming period.

N.B. - The blooming periods of flowers can vary depending on latitude, elevation and the weather. The dates provided in the descriptions are meant to serve as general guidelines only.

Remember that flowers are wildlife and should be treated as such. Many species have been seriously depleted due to loss of habitat and over-picking. In many areas, once-abundant species are now rare. Bring along a sketchbook and camera to record the flowers you see instead of picking them. This will help ensure there are more blossoms for you and others to enjoy in years to come.

FLOWER STRUCTURE

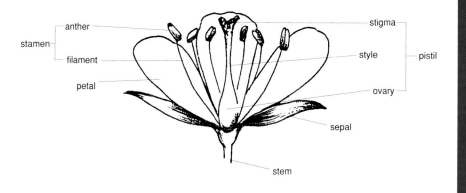

FLOWER SHAPES

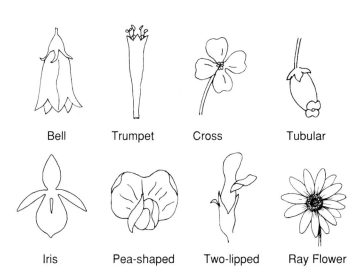

Bell   Trumpet   Cross   Tubular

Iris   Pea-shaped   Two-lipped   Ray Flower

WHITE FLOWERS

WILD CALLA
Calla palustris

Size: To 10 in. (25 cm)
Description: Thick-stemmed plant has heart-shaped leathery leaves. Tiny greenish flowers bloom in a cluster at the stem tip and are surrounded by a showy white spathe (modified leaf). Flowers bloom in summer and are succeeded by red berries.
Habitat: Bogs, muskegs, ponds.
Comments: Plant grows in shady bogs throughout the Northern Hemisphere. The entire plant is poisonous and should not be handled.

PUSSYTOES
Antennaria spp.

Size: To 8 in. (20 cm)
Description: Mat-forming plant has woolly stalks supporting fluffy flowerheads. Oval leaves are clustered at the plant base. Blooms June-July.
Habitat: Dry woodlands, open areas.
Comments: Several related species are found in Alaska ranging in color from pink to white.

ALASKA SPIRAEA
Spiraea beauverdiana

Size: To 30 in. (76 cm)
Description: Small shrub has thin red-brown branches. Leaves are toothed at the tip. Delicate white flowers bloom in flat-topped clusters June-July. Shiny brown seed heads persist into winter.
Habitat: Tundra, muskegs, wooded slopes, alpine meadows.
Comments: Leaves can be brewed to make tea.

DIAPENSIA
Diapensia lapponicum

Size: To 1 in. (2.5 cm)
Description: Low-growing plant has tough, oval leaves growing in small tussocks. Cup-shaped, 5-petalled white flowers bloom May-June.
Habitat: Alpine areas and tundra.
Comments: Hardy plant often found on rocky ledges and gravelly soils.

SINGLE DELIGHT
Moneses uniflora

Size: To 6 in. (15 cm)
Description: Naked flowering stalk rises from a rosette of round, toothed leaves. Nodding, 5-petalled white flower has a protruding pistil. Blooms June-July.
Habitat: Woodlands.
Comments: Fragrant plant is also called wood nymph and waxflower.

ALP LILY
Llyodia serotina

Size: To 6 in. (15 cm)
Description: Single, funnel-shaped white flower blooms atop a narrow stem. Narrow, grass-like basal leaves may be as long as the stem.
Habitat: High alpine areas on rocky soils.
Comments: Plant stores food in underground bulbs that allow it to survive long winters.

TWISTED STALK
Streptopus amplexifolius

Size: To 4 ft. (1.2 m)
Description: Tall plant has large alternate leaves clasping a crooked stem. White, bell-shaped flowers bloom at the end of 'kinked' stalks June-July and are succeeded by bright red berries.
Habitat: Tundra, rocky ridges, open forests.
Comments: Common and widespread throughout Alaska, it is one of four species of streptopus found here.

COASTAL STRAWBERRY
Fragaria chiloensis

Size: To 8 in. (20 cm)
Description: Mat-forming plant has coarsely-toothed, leathery leaves with three leaflets. Crisp white flowers bloom June-July and are succeeded in late summer by the familiar fruit.
Habitat: Coastal areas in southcentral and southeast Alaska.
Comments: The similar wild strawberry (*F. virginiana*) is found in the interior and eastern Alaska.

WILD CELERY
Angelica lucida

Size: To 3 ft. (91 cm)
Description: Stout plant has compound leaves with 3 toothed lobes. Thick, hollow stem supports numerous small clusters of white flowers arranged in an umbrella-like cluster. Blooms June-July.
Habitat: Coastal areas, river valleys, ditches, subalpine meadows.
Comments: An edible plant, it can be easily confused with the similar poison water hemlock (*Cicuta mackenzieana*).

GOATSBEARD
Aruncus sylvester

Size: To 4 ft. (1.2 m)
Description: Large compound leaves usually have 7 leaflets. Creamy flowers bloom in long, nodding spikes June-July, giving the plant its characteristic appearance.
Habitat: Moist woodlands, ravines, along waterways.
Comments: Most common in coastal areas.

THREE-LEAVED FOAMFLOWER
Tiarella trifoliata

Size: To 20 in. (51 cm)
Description: Perennial has long stemmed leaves with 3, irregular, coarsely-toothed lobes. Tiny white flowers bloom along slender flowering stalks
Habitat: Moist, shady forests to sub-alpine elevations.
Comments: At a distance, the small flowers look like flecks of foam on the surrounding leaves.

BUNCHBERRY
Cornus canadensis

Size: To 8 in. (20 cm)
Description: Low-growing shrub has erect stems with a whorl of 4-6 leaves at their tip. White flowers bloom in June-July and are succeeded by a small bunch of orange-red berries in late summer.
Habitat: Woodlands, tundra, alpine areas.
Comments: A common understory species in interior forests. Also called dwarf dogwood, it is one of 3 similar species found in Alaska.

LEATHERLEAF
Chamaedaphne calyculata

Size: To 3 ft. (91 cm)
Description: Low to medium-sized shrub has narrow leathery leaves with rolled edges. Leaves are greenish in summer and brownish in winter. White, urn-shaped flowers bloom in May.
Habitat: Muskegs, bogs, forests.
Comments: Often forms dense thickets in bogs and muskegs.

LABRADOR TEA
Ledum groenlandicum

Size: To 30 in. (76 cm)
Description: Evergreen, branching shrub has rusty hairs along its twigs and on the undersides of its leaves. Narrow leaves have edges rolled under. Showy white flowers have long stamens and bloom in umbrella-like clusters in June.
Habitat: Muskegs, bogs and woodlands in central and southern Alaska.
Comments: The closely related narrow-leaf labrador tea (*L. decumbens*) differs in that it is smaller (to 20 in./51 cm) and has narrower leaves. The dried leaves of both can be brewed to make tea.

BUCKBEAN
Menyanthes trifoliata

Size: To 12 in. (30 cm)
Description: Plant usually grows in water and has leathery, 3-part leaves. 'Bearded,' star-like white flowers bloom in a spike along leafless stalks May-June.
Habitat: Muskeg-bogs, lakes.
Comments: Also called bogbean, water shamrock and bognut, it is easily spotted in wet areas.

MOSS HEATHER
Cassiope stelleriana

Size: To 8 in. (20 cm)
Description: Mat-forming plant has scale-like leaves pressed flat against the stem to prevent water loss in high winds. White, bell-shaped, nodding flowers bloom June-July.
Habitat: Tundra, alpine and subalpine areas.
Comments: One of four similar species found in Alaska.

DEATH CAMAS
Zygadenus elegans

Size: To 36 in. (90 cm)
Description: Long grass-like leaves are clustered near the stem base. White, star-shaped flowers with green centers bloom in a long cluster June-August.
Habitat: Open woods, mountain meadows.
Comments: Plant contains a toxic poison in its leaves and bulbs and should never be handled.

GOLD THREAD
Coptis trifolia

Size: To 4 in. (10 cm)
Description: Lustrous basal leaves are toothed and have 3 lobes. Brilliant white, 5-petalled flowers bloom atop slender, naked stems June-July.
Habitat: Bogs, wet woods.
Comments: Plant was named for its thread-like, yellow underground stem.

STARFLOWER
Trientalis europea

Size: To 6 in. (15 cm)
Description: A whorl of 5-6 lance-shaped leaves grow near the top of slender stems. 1-3 stems arise from the whorl and each supports a single star-shaped flower. Blooms June-July.
Habitat: Muskegs, wet forests, tundra.
Comments: A shade-loving plant common south of the Brooks Range.

YARROW
Achillea millefolium

Size: To 2 ft. (60 cm)
Description: A long, unbranched stem supports dense clusters of round, yellow-centered daisy-like flowers. Each flower has four to six white (occasionally pinkish) rays. The unusual fern-like leaves are a good field mark. Blooms July-August.
Habitat: Dry open woods, roadsides, alpine meadows.
Comments: An aromatic herb, it is also known as milfoil. Often used in tea.

NARCISSUS ANEMONE
Anemone narcissiflora

Size: To 14 in. (36 cm)
Description: Erect, hairy plant has lobed leaves divided into narrow segments. Showy, yellow-centered flowers bloom June-August.
Habitat: Tundra, alpine meadows, open woodlands.
Comments: Several similar species of anemone are found in Alaska.

NORTHERN BEDSTRAW
Galium boreale

Size: To 20 in. (51 cm)
Description: Erect, branching plant
has leaves growing in whorls of 4
along square stems. Small clusters of
tiny white flowers bloom July-
August.
Habitat: Meadows, woods, thickets.
Comments: Plant foliage was once
prized as sweet-scented mattress
stuffing.

COW PARSNIP
Heracleum lanatum

Size: To 10 ft. (3 m)
Description: A large, conspicuous
plant. Deeply-lobed leaves grow
along the length of its thick, hollow
stem. Dense, flattened clusters of
creamy white flowers bloom July-
August.
Habitat: Common in moist fields and
woods.
Comments: It contains an alkaloid
that can severely irritate the skin of
some individuals. Resembles similar
plants, like the water hemlock, which
are deadly.

WHITE CLOVER
Trifolium repens

Size: To 12 in. (30 cm)
Description: Long-stemmed, dark
green leaves have three oval leaflets
and grow densely along creeping,
mat-forming stems. Rounded white
flowers bloom April-September.
Habitat: Common in fields, lawns
and disturbed areas.
Comments: The common lawn
clover, it is an excellent nectar
producer and a favorite of bees. Red
clover is also found in Alaska.

ARROW-LEAVED COLTSFOOT
Petasites saggitatus

Size: To 12 in. (30 cm)
Description: Distinguished by large, arrow-shaped basal leaves. Tiny white flowers bloom in terminal clusters in May-June and are succeeded by tufts of cottony seeds.
Habitat: Common on wet soils in eastern and central Alaska.
Comments: Two other similar species of coltsfoot are common in Alaska.

COTTON GRASS
Eriophorum spp.

Size: To 24 in. (61 cm)
Description: Long leaves are stiff and grass-like. Triangular stem supports one or more fluffy seed heads with long, silky hairs. Blooms June-July.
Habitat: Tundra, bogs, ditches.
Comments: There are several species of cotton grass in Alaska which look similar to one another.

MOUSE EAR CHICKWEED
Cerastrium arvense

Size: To 10 in. (25 cm)
Description: Mat-forming plant has slender, hairy leaves and white flowers with 5 notched petals. Blooms June-July.
Habitat: Coastal and alpine areas, dry slopes, roadsides.
Comments: Considered a weed by most, it is edible and often cooked as a spinach substitute. This introduced species was at one time fed extensively to chickens.

GRASS OF PARNASSUS
Parnassia palustris

Size: To 15 in. (38 cm)
Description: Basal leaves are yellow-green and heart-shaped. A single leaf clasps the stem below its middle. Showy, star-shaped flowers bloom at stem tips July-August.
Habitat: Meadows, wet open areas throughout most of Alaska.
Comments: Also called bog star, it is one of 3 related species found in Alaska.

YELLOW, ORANGE AND GREEN FLOWERS

COMMON MONKEYFLOWER
Mimulus guttatus

Size: To 5 ft. (1.5 m)
Description: Trumpet-shaped yellow flowers have dark-spotted, hairy throats. Oval leaves are coarsely toothed; lower leaves are stalked, upper ones are clasping. Flowers bloom in loose terminal clusters July-August.
Habitat: Wet areas, meadows, and ditches at most elevations.
Comments: Purple monkeyflowers are also found in Alaska.

YELLOW DRYAS
Dryas drummondii

Size: To 10 in. (25 cm)
Description: Low matted plant has oval leaves with prominent veins. Solitary, pale yellow, nodding flowers bloom June-July. Flowers are replaced by fluffy 'heads' comprised of seeds with feathery plumes.
Habitat: Gravelly soils, rocky slopes.
Comments: Also called mountain avens, its leathery, evergreen leaves are distinctive. Two similar white-flowered dryas (*D. octopetala* and *D. integrifolia)* are also found in Alaska.

WOOLLY MULLEIN
Verbascum thapsus

Size: To 6 ft. (1.8 m)
Description: Tall leafy plant that tapers from a broad base to a slender spike of yellow flowers. Flowers bloom a few at a time throughout summer.
Habitat: Roadsides and open areas.
Comments: Miners used to make torches from these plants by dipping them in tallow.

YELLOW POND LILY
Nuphar polysepalum

Size: To 3 in. (8 cm)
Description: Aquatic plant has large heart-shaped leaves with long stalks. Bulbous yellow flower blooms during summer.
Habitat: Ponds and sluggish streams.
Comments: Widely used by native people as a source of food, the roots were eaten boiled or roasted and the seeds popped like popcorn. Also called waterlily and spatterdock.

TOADFLAX
Linaria vulgaris

Size: To 3 ft. (91 cm)
Description: Upright blue-green plant has narrow leaves growing along the entire stem. Yellow, spurred flowers have a patch of orange in the throat that acts as a nectar guide for insects and hummingbirds. Blooms July-August.
Habitat: Roadsides, waste areas.
Comments: A non-native plant that has become widespread.

YELLOW OXYTROPE
Oxytropis campestris

Size: To 10 in. (25 cm)
Description: Low plant has basal
leaves with numerous oval leaflets.
Yellow, pea-shaped flowers bloom in
terminal clusters May-June.
Habitat: Roadsides, gravelly and
sandy soils.
Comments: Also called locoweed, it
contains a toxin that causes loss of
muscle control. One of several
similar species of purple and yellow
oxytrope found in Alaska.

SHRUBBY CINQUEFOIL
Potentilla fruticosa

Size: To 3 ft. (90 cm)
Description: Small, woody shrub
with reddish, shredding bark and
yellow flowers. Toothed leaves have
three or five lobes. Blooms June-
August.
Habitat: Tundra, bogs, alpine slopes.
Comments: Widely cultivated as an
ornamental, it is one of several
cinquefoils found in Alaska.

STREAM VIOLET
Viola glabella

Size: To 12 in. (30 cm)
Description: Yellow flower has
conspicuous dark veins on three of
its five petals. Heart-shaped leaves
have sharply pointed tips. Blooms
June-July.
Habitat: Moist forests, clearings
and near streams at low to middle
elevations.
Comments: Several other species
of mauve, blue, yellow and white
violets are found in Alaska.

ALASKA POPPY
Papaver alaskanum

Size: To 8 in. (10 cm)
Description: Small, lobed leaves are clustered near plant base and dead leaves often persist on stems. Delicate 4-petalled yellow flowers bloom June-July.
Habitat: Gravelly soils.
Comments: One of several species of yellow poppy found in Alaska.

NORTHERN GREEN BOG ORCHID
Plantanthera hyperborea

Size: To 16 in. (41 cm)
Description: Narrow leaves with linear veins grow along the entire stem length. Small, greenish orchids bloom along the stem in July.
Habitat: Wet meadows, bogs, moist woods.
Comments: Hybridizes commonly with the similar, white-flowered bog candle (*P. dilatata*).

INDIAN HELLEBORE
Veratrum viride

Size: To 6 ft. (1.8 m)
Description: Tall, hairy plant has large leaves with parallel veins. Greenish flowers bloom in long, often drooping, spikes June-August.
Habitat: Wet woods, alpine meadows.
Comments: An extremely poisonous plant that is used medicinally by many native and European cultures. Extracts of the plant have been used as insecticides.

CHOCOLATE LILY
Fritillaria camschatcensis

Size: To 18 in. (46 cm)
Description: Perennial plant has whorls of narrow leaves growing along the stem. Green-brown bell-shaped flowers bloom June-July.
Habitat: Wet woods, meadows.
Comments: Also called northern rice root, its rice-like roots are edible sources of starch and sugar.

ESCHSCHOLTZ BUTTERCUP
Ranunculus eschscholtzii

Size: To 8 in. (20 cm)
Description: Shiny, yellow flower with five overlapping petals. Leaves are oval and usually have 3 lobes. Blooms May-June.
Habitat: Mountain meadows, rocky slopes, along waterways.
Comments: Many similar species of buttercups are found in Alaska. All are poisonous.

MARSH MARIGOLD
Caltha palustris

Size: To 30 in. (76 cm)
Description: Glistening leaves are round or heart-shaped and have gently toothed edges. Bright yellow flowers have 5-7 petal-like sepals.
Habitat: Wetlands, streams, marshes.
Comments: The plant leaves are often eaten cooked, but are poisonous when raw. The similar, white-flowered mountain marigold (*C. leptosepala*) is found in similar habitats.

COMMON DANDELION
Taraxacum officinale

Size: To 12 in. (30 cm)
Description: Told by its elongate, toothed leaves and shaggy yellow flowers that bloom frequently throughout the growing season. Tufts of whitish, hairy seeds succeed the flowers and are dispersed by the wind.
Habitat: Abundant in open and grassy areas.
Comments: The leaves are often used in salads and the blossoms for wine-making. There are 15 species of *Taraxacum* native to Alaska.

COMMON PLANTAIN
Plantago major

Size: To 20 in. (50 cm)
Description: Large, tough basal leaves are finely-toothed with deep longitudinal veins. Tiny greenish flowers bloom in slender spikes arising from the leafy base.
Habitat: Open areas, roadsides, waste areas.
Comments: An introduced weed that is widespread in towns and fields.

HORSETAIL
Equisetum spp.

Size: To 2 ft. (60 cm)
Description: Slender, jointed stems have whorls of thin branches. Separate pinkish stems arise with a spore-producing 'cone' at their tip.
Habitat: Moist woodlands, roadsides, swamps.
Comments: Common in wet areas throughout Alaska. The mare's tail (*Hippus vulgaris*) is found in similar habitats and resembles a tiny spruce tree.

RED AND PINK FLOWERS

BOG ROSEMARY
Andromeda polifolia

Size: To 12 in. (30 cm)
Description: Shrubby, evergreen plant has narrow leaves with rolled edges. Pinkish urn-shaped flowers bloom May-June.
Habitat: Bogs, wet woods, alpine areas.
Comments: Often grows in association with cassiopes and other mat-forming plants. Entire plant is poisonous.

FIREWEED
Epilobium angustifolium

Size: To 7 ft. (2 m)
Description: Distinguished at a glance by its long conical spike of bright pink, 4-petalled flowers. Blooms July-August.
Habitat: Open woodlands, clearings and meadows.
Comments: Often grows in dense colonies and blankets hillsides and meadows. The shorter, some-times sprawling dwarf fireweed (*E. latifolium*; to 20 in./51 cm) is common along waterways and mountain slopes throughout most of Alaska.

INDIAN PAINTBRUSH
Castilleja spp.

Size: To 3 ft. (90 cm)
Description: Ragged red, yellow, pink or purple wildflower often grows in dense colonies. Tiny flowers are hidden within colorful, petal-like bracts (modified leaves). Blooms March-October.
Habitat: Woodlands and mountain meadows.
Comments: Related to snapdragons, they are often parasitic, living off nutrients absorbed from the roots of other plants.

GROUND CONE
Boschniakia rossica

Size: To 12 in. (30 cm)
Description: Distinctive parasite resembles an upright, reddish pine cone. Tiny reddish flowers bloom June-July.
Habitat: Wet woods, along waterways.
Comments: Also called broomrape, it is parasitic on the roots of the green alder throughout most of its range.

RED COLUMBINE
Aquilegia formosa

Size: To 3 ft. (91 cm)
Description: Branching perennial plant has stunning red-and-yellow, nodding flowers. Blooms June-July.
Habitat: Open woodlands, meadows.
Comments: Each of the plant's petals stretches back into a long spur. Blue columbine (*A. brevistyla*) is also found in Alaska.

ROSEROOT
Sedum rosea

Size: To 12 in. (30 cm)
Description: Mat-forming plant has stems covered with fleshy leaves. Small, red to purple flowers bloom in dense clusters at stem tips in June.
Habitat: Alpine areas, tundra, rocky ridges.
Comments: Able to survive harsh and/or arid conditions since its leaves store water. Also called king's crown.

ALPINE AZALEA
Loiseleuria procumbens

Size: To 6 in. (15 cm)
Description: Mat-forming evergreen shrub has stems covered with small, oval opposite leaves. Clusters of small, 5-petalled flowers bloom at stem tips in June.
Habitat: Alpine areas, rocky ridges, coastal bogs.
Comments: Often grows in association with white-flowered diapensia and other dwarf shrubs.

ESKIMO POTATO
Hedysarum alpinum

Size: To 3 ft. (91 cm)
Description: Long compound leaves have 9-21 leaflets. Pea-shaped, pink to purple flowers bloom in a flowing terminal cluster in June-July.
Habitat: Open forests, rocky slopes, roadsides.
Comments: The roots were an important food source for Native cultures who ate them raw, boiled or roasted. Is similar to the poisonous wild sweet pea (*H. boreale mackenzii*) which has shorter flower spikes.

PRICKLY ROSE
Rosa acicularis

Size: To 6 ft. (1.8 m)
Description: A prickly shrub with broad, pink, five-petalled, sweet-smelling flowers. Blooms June-July.
Habitat: Open areas and woodlands at middle to upper elevations.
Comments: Flowers are succeeded by fruits called 'hips' that are rich in vitamin C and often used in jellies, jams and teas. The similar nootka rose (*R. nutkana*) is also common in Alaska.

SHOOTING STAR
Dodecatheon pulchellum

Size: To 20 in. (50 cm)
Description: Graceful plant with drooping, dart-like reddish flowers with inverted petals exposing yellow stamen tubes. Blooms in June.
Habitat: Moist soils in meadows, fields and open woodlands.
Comments: The smaller frigid shooting star (*D. frigidum*) is found in alpine meadows throughout most of Alaska.

TWINFLOWER
Linnaea borealis

Size: To 2 ft. (61 cm)
Description: Trailing shrub has rounded, opposite, evergreen leaves. Slender stems support nodding pairs of pink, bell-shaped flowers. Blooms May-July.
Habitat: Moist woods.
Comments: Flowers are sweetly fragrant. Plant was named after the famous botanical taxonomist Carolus Linnaeus.

ARCTIC DOCK
Rumex arcticus

Size: To 4 ft. (1.2 m)
Description: Tall, red plant has elongate leaves. Tiny flowers are hidden beneath red or green bracts.
Habitat: Wet areas.
Comments: One of several species of dock found in Alaska. All have sour-tasting leaves that are prized as cooking greens.

COMMON FLEABANE
Erigeron philadelphicus

Size: To 2 ft. (61 cm)
Description: Narrow leaves clasp the stem and are densely clustered at the plant base. Pink to white ray flowers bloom in loose clusters June-August.
Habitat: Moist meadows, open woods.
Comments: One of several fleabanes found in Alaska. The plants were once hung in houses to keep fleas away. Similar to asters, the flower rays are narrower and more numerous.

ROUND-LEAVED SUNDEW
Drosera rotundifolia

Size: To 12 in. (30 cm)
Description: Rounded basal leaves are covered with reddish, sticky droplets. White to pink, 5-petalled flowers bloom in a terminal cluster July-August.
Habitat: Bogs.
Comments: A carnivorous plant that feeds on the bugs that are attracted to, and entrapped by, the sweet, sticky fluid excreted by its leaves.

BLUE AND PURPLE FLOWERS

Alaska's State Flower

ALPINE FORGET-ME-NOT
Myosotis alpestris

Size: To 12 in. (30 cm)
Description: Elongate leaves are covered with stiff hairs. Bright blue, 5-petalled, yellow-centered flowers bloom May-June.
Habitat: Mountain slopes and meadows, alpine tundra.
Comments: Flowers were once worn to maintain a lover's affection.

INKY GENTIAN
Gentiana glauca

Size: To 6 in. (15 cm)
Description: Stiff plant has a basal rosette of spoon-shaped leaves. Greenish-blue, tubular flowers with accordion-like folds in their sides bloom July-August.
Habitat: Alpine areas.
Comments: One of several species of gentian found in Alaska.

ARCTIC LUPINE
Lupinus arcticus

Size: To 20 in. (50 cm)
Description: Tall perennial has compound leaves with 6-8 leaflets. Bluish, pea-like flowers bloom in an elongate cluster June-July.
Habitat: Moist soils in meadows and forests.
Comments: Though poisonous to people, their seeds are a valuable food source for grouse and ptarmigan. The similar nootka lupine (*L. nootkaensis*) is common in southern Alaska.

MONKSHOOD
Aconitum columbianum

Size: To 6 ft. (1.8 m)
Description: A slender, leafy plant with deep blue flowers resembling a monk's habit. Leaves usually have 5 deeply divided lobes. Blooms July-September.
Habitat: Mountain meadows, moist woods.
Comments: Often grows in dense vegetation. A highly toxic plant, it should not be handled.

TALL LARKSPUR
Delphinium glaucum

Size: To 6 ft. (1.8 m)
Description: Tall plant has large leaves with 5 deeply divided lobes. The flowering stem is often purplish and supports a terminal cluster of purplish, 5-part flowers with prominent spurs. Blooms July-August.
Habitat: Moist open woods, meadows.
Comments: Plant is poisonous to livestock and people. Seeds are highly toxic.

SIBERIAN ASTER
Aster sibiricus

Size: To 12 in. (30 cm)
Description: Narrow leaves grow alternately along stem. Purple, yellow-centered starburst flowers bloom July-August.
Habitat: Woodlands, meadows, along waterways.
Comments: One of several species of aster found in Alaska. All have similar starburst flower heads.

HAREBELL
Campanula rotundifolia

Size: To 38 in. (1 m)
Description: Plant with grass-like leaves and a drooping cluster of pale blue to lavender, bell-shaped flowers. Basal leaves are heart-shaped. Blooms July-August.
Habitat: Grassy and rocky slopes, dry open woods.
Comments: Also called Scotch bluebell, it is one of several similar species that occur in Alaska.

PURPLE MOUNTAIN SAXIFRAGE
Saxifraga oppositifolia

Size: To 2 in. (5 cm)
Description: Mat-forming plant has scale-like leaves clasping the stems along their entire length. Showy purple or lilac 5-petalled flowers bloom singly at stem tips May-June.
Habitat: Rocky alpine areas, exposed tundra.
Comments: Saxifrages were once thought to have the curative power to dissolve gallstones, remove freckles and relieve toothaches.

WILD IRIS
Iris setosa

Size: To 24 in. (60 cm)
Description: Tall plant has long, narrow leaves and a thick flower stalk. Large, showy, 9-part blue to purple flowers bloom June-July.
Habitat: Bogs, meadows, wet woods.
Comments: Flower has 3 large outer petal-like sepals, 3 upright petals and 3 crest-like branches of the seed pod. The entire plant is poisonous.

BLUEBELLS
Mertensia paniculata

Size: To 30 in. (76 cm)
Description: Hairy, oval to lance-shaped leaves grow along length of branching stem. Clusters of distinctive blue, nodding flowers bloom in open clusters June-July.
Habitat: Meadows, beaches and woodlands.
Comments: Also called lungwort and chiming bells. Flowers are occasionally pink or white.

WILD BLUE FLAX
Linum perenne

Size: To 24 in. (60 cm)
Description: Wiry plant has narrow, slightly hairy, grass-like leaves. Purple to blue, 5-petalled flowers bloom in June-July.
Habitat: Dry slopes, sandy soils.
Comments: Tough stems were used once used for weaving ropes and cloth. Seeds are a source of linseed oil.

ALASKA REGIONS

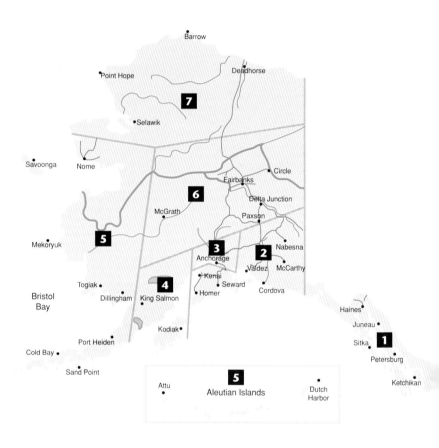

1	SOUTHEAST ALASKA
2	SOUTHCENTRAL ALASK▪
3	ANCHORAGE & VICINIT
4	SOUTHWEST ALASKA
5	WESTERN ALASKA
6	CENTRAL ALASKA
7	NORTHERN ALASKA

1 SOUTHEAST ALASKA

Also called the Alaska Panhandle, the area is dominated by rainforests of spruce, hemlock and cedar. At upper elevations, the trees are replaced by alpine tundra and vast icefields. The famous Inside Passage is a marine highway along the coast that offers spectacular views of the coastal fjords, mountains and glaciers. Abundant species include sitka black-tailed deer, bald eagles, bears, harbor seals, whales and porpoises.

2 SOUTHCENTRAL ALASKA

The region encompasses the varied terrain ranging from coastal forests and alpine areas, to interior tundra, muskegs and mixed hardwood forests.

3 ANCHORAGE AND VICINITY

Anchorage is home to approximately half of the state's population and is the gateway to many of its outstanding natural attractions.

4 SOUTHWEST ALASKA

Prominent attractions found here include the state's largest lake (Iliamna), its largest island (Kodiak) and the internationally-famous bear-watching area at the McNeil River State Game Sanctuary. The brown bears found on Kodiak Island are the world's largest land carnivores.

5 WESTERN ALASKA

Much of western Alaska is covered by treeless tundra, although forests and shrub thickets persist in many areas.

The thousand-mile long chain of Aleutian Islands are treeless and covered with grassy meadows and tundra. Puffins, sea otters and brown bears are a few of the area's most prominent wildlife species. The world's largest run of sockeye salmon occurs here, and millions of birds nest on the Yukon Delta each year. Roads are few and far between, and most places are accessed via boat or plane.

6 CENTRAL ALASKA

The rolling, often mountainous landscape in this region is dominated by forests comprised of spruce and hardwoods including birch, alder and poplar. Boggy muskegs are found at lower elevations throughout the area. Abundant species include moose, bears, wolves, porcupines, beavers, waterfowl and songbirds. Dall sheep, marmots, eagles and pikas are found at upper elevations.

7 NORTHERN ALASKA

Within this region, stunted trees give way to the treeless, wind-swept tundra. During summer, the area is dotted with thousands of lakes formed from snow melt. The spongy ground supports a limited number of plants including mosses, lichens, grasses and wildflowers. Millions of birds migrate here in summer to feed on abundant insects.

SOUTHEAST ALASKA

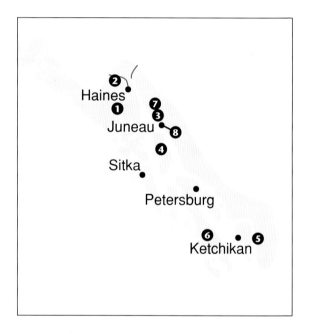

Haines

Juneau

Sitka

Petersburg

Ketchikan

Parks/Wildlife Areas

❶ GLACIER BAY NATIONAL PARK AND PRESERVE
One of the state's most scenic areas features a dozen tidewater glaciers, countless fjords and the snow-capped mountains of the Fairweather range. Over 200 species of birds are found here, and marine mammals are also abundant. Area is only accessible by plane or boat and accommodations are available on site.
Location: Northwest of Juneau
Phone: (907) 697-2230

❷ CHILKAT BALD EAGLE PRESERVE
One of the world's largest concentration of bald eagles – up to 4,500 birds – gathers here between October and February to feed on a late run of salmon in the Chilkat River.
Location: Near Haines
Phone: (907) 465-4563

❸ MENDENHALL WETLANDS STATE GAME REFUGE
Meltwater from the glacier has created a 3,600-acre tidal estuary home to over 140 species of birds. Popular birding, hiking, and hunting destination.
Location: Juneau
Phone: (907) 465-4359

❹ ADMIRALTY ISLAND - PACK CREEK
Bears outnumber people on this lush coastal island that also boasts the world's largest concentration of nesting bald eagles. The Pack Creek sanctuary features a bear observation tower. Accessed via boat or floatplane from Juneau or Sitka. Permits must be obtained in advance.
Location: South of Juneau
Phone: (907) 586-8751

❺ MISTY FJORDS NATIONAL MONUMENT
Coastal rainforest harbors species including bears, deer and wolves. Surrounding craggy cliffs and snow-capped peaks abruptly rise 3,000 ft. above the ocean. One highlight is New Eddystone Rock, a towering volcanic plug. Accessed via boat or plane.
Location: East of Ketchikan
Phone: (907) 225-2148

❻ PRINCE OF WALES ISLAND
The third largest island in the U.S. supports large populations of deer, bears and eagles. Extensive limestone areas are honeycombed by caves and sinkholes. A number of viewing platforms allow visitors to observe spawning salmon.
Location: West of Ketchikan
Phone: (907) 826-3271

Museums/Attractions

❼ MENDENHALL GLACIER
One of the state's most accessible glaciers is a river of ice 22 miles long that ends in Mendenhall Lake. Trails on both sides of the glacier offer scenic views of the area. Visitor center.
Location: North of Juneau
Phone: (907) 789-0097

❽ GASTINEAU SALMON HATCHERY
State-of-the-art facility hatches more than 160 million salmon eggs annually. Saltwater aquarium highlights nearshore sea life.
Location: Juneau
Phone: (907) 463-5114

SOUTHCENTRAL ALASKA

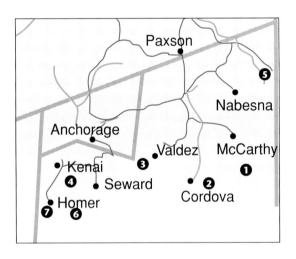

Parks/Wildlife Areas

❶ WRANGELL – ST. ELIAS NATIONAL PARK & PRESERVE
The country's largest national park covers 13 million acres of mountainous and coastal habitat and encompasses 9 of the 16 highest peaks in North America and the continent's largest glacier. Backcountry travellers should plan their outings carefully since access is limited and trails are not maintained. Visitor center provides trip-planning assistance.
Location: East of Valdez
Phone: (907) 822-5234

❷ COPPER RIVER DELTA
Huge estuary nearly 50 miles long is an important staging area for up to 20 million migrating birds each year. Bears, weasels, wolverines, otters, muskrats, beavers and wolves also forage in the area. Peak migration period is April-May.
Location: Southeast of Cordova
Phone: (907) 424-3215

❸ PRINCE WILLIAM SOUND
One of the state's most scenic and popular areas, it encompasses islands, glaciers, forests, rivers, lakes, mountains, wetlands and muskegs. Abundant wildlife species include bald eagles, deer, otters, sea lions, whales and sea birds.
Location: Northeast of Seward
Phone: (907) 745-5015

❹ KENAI NATIONAL WILDLIFE REFUGE
Expansive mountainous refuge is noted for its hundreds of lakes and abundant wildlife including moose, bears, Dall sheep, loons and bald eagles.
Location: East of Kenai
Phone: (907) 262-7021

❺ TETLIN NATIONAL WILDLIFE REFUGE
Refuge encompasses a wide range of habitats including thickets, muskegs, spruce and hardwood forests, wetlands and riparian areas. Bald eagles, loons, ospreys, beavers, bears and moose are a few of the common species found here. Visitor amenities include campgrounds, nature trails and a viewing platform.
Location: NE of Nabesna
Phone: (907) 883-5312

❻ KENAI FJORDS NATIONAL PARK
Glaciers have gouged deep fjords along the coastal part of this park. The interior has broad mountain valleys and encompasses Harding Icefield, the fourth largest in the nation. Common species include moose, marmots, guillemots, puffins, murrelets, eagles, sea lions, seals, humpback whales and sea otters. Visitor center is in Seward.
Location: South of Seward
Phone: (907) 224-3175

❼ KACHEMAK BAY STATE PARK AND WILDERNESS AREA
Area encompasses one of the world's richest marine environments. Homer Spit – one of the world's longest natural gravel bars – juts out nearly five miles into the bay and forms a protective breakwater. Millions of migrating birds pass through the area each year and marine mammals and sea birds are common.
Location: Homer
Phone: (907) 235-7024

ANCHORAGE & VICINITY

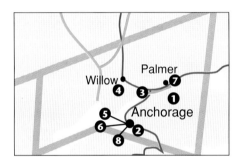

Parks/Wildlife Areas

❶ CHUGACH STATE PARK

Mountainous park on the out-skirts of Anchorage is home to moose, bears, wolves, wolverines, Dall sheep and numerous species of birds. Several roads lead from the city directly into the park. A popular hiking and camping des-tination for both residents and tourists. State-owned wilderness cabins can be rented in the park. Visitor center.
Location: Anchorage
Phone: (907) 345-5014

❷ ANCHORAGE COASTAL WILDLIFE REFUGE

Critical waterfowl habitat is one of the state's most easily acces-sible and scenic refuges. Marsh and tidal flat habitats support over 130 resident and migratory species. Naturalists are often present and boardwalks feature interpretive signs.
Location: Anchorage
Phone: (907) 269-8700

❸ PALMER HAY FLATS STATE GAME REFUGE

The wet meadows and marshes found here are important habi-tats for tens of thousands of ducks, swans and geese. Waterfowl are most abundant in spring.
Location: Palmer
Phone: (907) 745-5015

❹ NANCY LAKE STATE RECREATION AREA

Beautiful rolling landscape fea-tures over 100 lakes noted for their abundance of trout and pike. A popular hiking, camping and canoeing destination. Cabins are available to rent.
Location: North of Anchorage
Phone: (907) 745-3975

❺ FAR NORTH BICENTENNIAL PARK

Sanctuary within the city limits highlights the common plants and animals found within promi-nent regional ecosystems. Trails are well-maintained throughout.
Location: Anchorage
Phone: (907) 267-1246

Museums/Attractions

❻ ALASKA ZOO

30-acre park highlights native animals and plants, many in natural settings.
Location: Anchorage
Phone: (907) 346-3242

❼ MUSKOX FARM

A domesticated herd of muskox is farmed here for their soft underhair – called qiviut – which Natives knit into warm clothing. Visitors can closely observe the animals from fenced walkways.
Location: Palmer
Phone: (907) 745-4151

❽ SHIP CREEK

Creek running through Anchorage is choked with spawning salmon during summer months. Watch their primordial journey from a viewing platform downtown, or at the Elmendorf State Hatchery located two miles upstream.
Location: Anchorage
Phone: (907) 343-4355

SOUTHWEST ALASKA

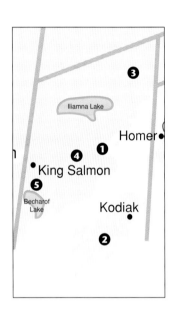

Parks/Wildlife Areas

❶ MCNEIL RIVER STATE GAME SANCTUARY

Visitors can watch up to 60 brown bears feed on spawning salmon at this world-famous sanctuary. Admission is by permit only, and permits are awarded in a lottery. Call for an application.
Location: West of Homer
Phone: (907) 267-2180

❷ KODIAK NATIONAL WILDLIFE REFUGE

Alaska's largest island is a haven for bears, eagles and sea birds. The Kodiak brown bear is the largest subspecies of grizzly and the largest land carnivore in the world. The area's forests, lakes, wetlands and meadows are home to an abundance of wildlife. Guided tours are available and public-use cabins are rented through a quarterly lottery.
Location: South of Kodiak
Phone: (907) 487-2600

❸ LAKE CLARK NATIONAL PARK AND PRESERVE

Active volcanic area provides excellent hiking and sightseeing opportunities. Mountain ranges in the park divide it into distinct regions of coastal plain on one side, and lake and tundra on the other. Marshes, grasslands, thickets, boreal forests, lakes and wetlands harbor swans, sea birds, bears, wolves and trophy-sized fishes. Lake Clark is one of the richest salmon habitats on earth.
Location: Northeast of Homer
Phone: (907) 781-2218

❹ KATMAI NATIONAL PARK AND PRESERVE

Area offers superlative scenery and the opportunity to see bears and salmon. Brooks Camp has two bear viewing platforms that allow visitors to observe the bears at close range. In 1912, a volcanic eruption 10 times as powerful as Mt. St. Helen's buried a valley within the park – known as the Valley of 10,000 Smokes – under a layer of ash up to 700 ft. thick. Accommodations are available in a lodge and campground in Brooks Camp; visitation has soared in recent years and reservations should be made well in advance.
Location: East of King Salmon
Phone: (907) 246-3305

❺ BECHAROF NATIONAL WILDLIFE REFUGE

1.2 million-acre refuge is dominated inland by rolling hills, tundra wetlands and Becharof Lake, the second largest in the state. Over 100,000 caribou winter here. Brown bears are common near streams during salmon spawning. Seals and sea birds are abundant on the south coastal area.
Location: South of King Salmon
Phone: (907) 246-3305

WESTERN ALASKA

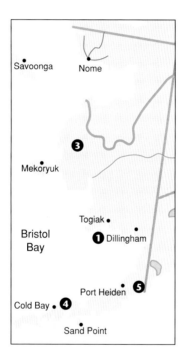

Savoonga

Nome

3

Mekoryuk

Togiak

1 Dillingham

Bristol
Bay

Port Heiden **5**

Cold Bay **4**

Sand Point

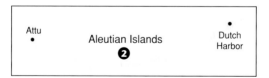

Attu

Aleutian Islands

2

Dutch
Harbor

Parks/Wildlife Areas

❶ WALRUS ISLANDS STATE GAME SANCTUARY

Seven small islands in Bristol Bay are the summer breeding grounds of up to 15,000 walruses. Steller sea lions, foxes and countless sea birds are also found here. You must register to gain access to the sanctuary.
Location: Bristol Bay
Phone: (907) 842-2334

❷ ALASKA MARITIME NATIONAL WILDLIFE REFUGE

Refuge encompasses hundreds of islands and land parcels in coastal waters and adjacent seas of Alaska including most of the Aleutian Islands and the remote Pribilof Islands. The Aleutians are the longest chain of small islands in the world and stretch for over 1,000 miles from the end of the Alaska Peninsula. The 124 islands in the chain are actually the tips of volcanic peaks; most are tree-less and support low growing shrubs and grasses. Called 'Cradle of the Storms' by Native Alaskans, the windswept islands are pounded by rain and snow more than half of the year. The Pribilof Islands are a cluster of islands north of the Aleutians. In summer, they are the breeding ground for thousands of seals and dozens of species of sea birds. There is regular air service to the major settlements on islands within the refuge.
Location: Coastal waters
Phone: (907) 235-6546

❸ YUKON DELTA NATIONAL WILDLIFE REFUGE

Massive delta refuge – the second largest in the nation – hosts up to 20 million migratory birds each year. Over 165 species of birds and 40 species of mammals are common in this lush habitat containing over 40,000 lakes. Herds of muskox and reindeer live on nearby Nunivak Island. Most of the refuge is owned by Native Alaskans and it is impor-tant to consult the refuge head-quarters in Bethel before plan-ning a trip.
Location: West-central coast
Phone: (907) 543-3151

❹ IZEMBEK NATIONAL WILDLIFE REFUGE

Located near the tip of the Alaska Peninsula, the area is an impor-tant migratory staging area for geese and ducks. Many migrants congregate in the massive 84,000 acre eelgrass bed in Izembeck Lagoon. Sea ducks winter in the refuge, and otters, seals and foxes reside year-round.
Location: Near Cold Bay
Phone: (907) 532-2445

❺ ANIAKCHAK NATIONAL MONUMENT AND PRESERVE

Centerpiece of monument is a huge crater 6 mi. (10 km) in diameter and 2,000 ft. (609 m) deep created by the collapse of a volcano. The caldera also features a lake heated by hot springs and a 2,200 ft. (670 m) cone.
Location: Near Port Heiden
Phone: (907) 532-2445

CENTRAL ALASKA

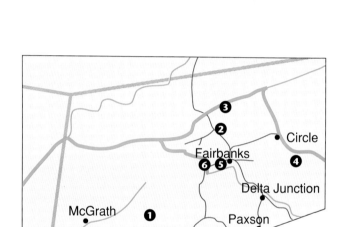

Parks/Wildlife Areas

❶ DENALI NATIONAL PARK AND PRESERVE

Perhaps no other area in Alaska better exemplifies the ruggedness and sheer beauty of the Alaskan wilderness. Expansive valleys are framed by glacier-strewn Alaska Range, with the towering Mount McKinley at its heart. Denali means 'the great one' in Tanaina Indian dialect. Abundant wildlife include caribou, wolves, moose, grizzly bears, foxes, dall sheep and ptarmigan. Excellent visitor center provides books, maps, bus coupons and a number of interpretive programs. Highlight is bus ride that travels the 85 mile (137 km) wilderness road from the park entrance to Wonder Lake. Hotels are available and should be booked well in advance of summer high season. Park campsites are available on a first-come, first-served basis. Park is reached by most via Anchorage by road, rail or air.
Location: NW of Anchorage
Phone: (907) 683-2294

❷ WHITE MOUNTAINS NATIONAL RECREATION AREA

Popular canoeing and hiking area features unusual limestone cliffs, subarctic caves and rocky pinnacles. Spruce-hardwood forests and muskegs are home to common species including moose, bears, marmots, pikas, dall sheep, lynx, hawks and owls. In summer, many visitors float the Beaver Creek National Wild and Scenic River.
Location: Fairbanks
Phone: (907) 474-7505

❸ YUKON FLATS NATIONAL WILDLIFE REFUGE

8.6 million acre refuge encompasses more than 400 lakes and in summer is host to the densest concentrations of nesting waterfowl found anywhere in the state. Access is via boat or plane.
Location: North of Fairbanks
Phone: (907) 456-0440

❹ YUKON – CHARLEY RIVERS NATIONAL PRESERVE

Beautiful, unspoiled wilderness area where the silty Yukon River flows through a huge geologic fault and is joined by a number of waterways including the Charley River. River floating is a popular way to view the area and its abundant wildlife.
Location: South of Circle
Phone: (907) 547-2233

❺ CREAMER'S FIELD MIGRATORY WATERFOWL REFUGE

An important nesting and migratory sanctuary for geese, cranes waterfowl, raptors and songbirds. Visitor center has numerous educational exhibits. Self-guided nature trails are posted with interpretive signs.
Location: Fairbanks
Phone: (907) 459-7213

Museums/Attractions

❻ UNIVERSITY MUSEUM

Features exhibits on the natural and cultural history of Alaska.
Location: Fairbanks
Phone: (907) 474-7505

NORTHERN ALASKA

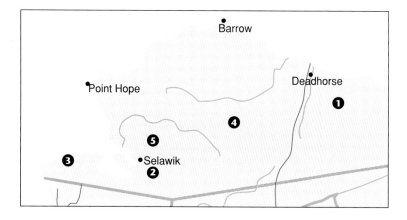

Parks/Wildlife Areas

❶ ARCTIC NATIONAL WILDLIFE REFUGE

Remote 19 million acre refuge is one of the few areas to contain completely undisturbed arctic ecosystems. The huge Porcupine caribou herd (180,000 + animals) migrates through and calves in the refuge each year. Over 170 kinds of birds are found here, including many circumpolar species. Bears, Dall sheep, wolves, swans and longspurs are a few of the species that await the adventurous back-country traveller. Area has no designated campsites or marked trails. Most visitors are flown in and out of the refuge.
Location: Northeast corner of Alaska
Phone: (907) 456-0250

❷ SELAWIK NATIONAL WILDLIFE REFUGE

The Arctic Circle splits this refuge of river deltas, estuaries and tundra habitats. Primarily a wetland, it is an extremely valuable staging and nesting area for over 175 species of birds. Caribou, moose, bears and wolves are also common.
Location: Near Selawik
Phone: (907) 442-3799

❸ BERING LAND BRIDGE NATIONAL PRESERVE

Area commemorates the once continuous land/ice bridge between Alaska and Siberia that allowed people and animals to reach North America. Animals found here include muskox, polar bears, caribou and moose. Serpentine Hot Springs is a pop-ular stopover for visitors. Recreational activities include camping, river floating and wildlife observation.
Location: East of Selawik
Phone: (907) 443-2522

❹ GATES OF THE ARCTIC NATIONAL PARK AND PRESERVE

Located north of the Arctic Circle, this remote wilderness encompasses glacial valleys, the scenic headland of the rugged Brooks Range, seven wild and scenic rivers and hundreds of lakes. Common wildlife includes moose, Dall sheep, wolves and raptors; hundreds of thousands of caribou migrate through the area each fall. Visitors should be self-sufficient and skilled in wilderness survival.
Location: NE of Selawik
Phone: (907) 456-0281

❺ KOBUK VALLEY NATIONAL PARK

Just north of the Arctic Circle, this 1.7 million-acre park is set in the heart of the arctic wilderness. The park encompasses the massive Great Kobuk Sand Dunes that were created by the grinding of glaciers. The Kobuk River which winds through the park is sought out by anglers and river-travellers. Common wildlife include bears, moose, wolves, foxes, wolverines, caribou, eagles and loons.
Location: Northeast of Selawik
Phone: (907) 442-3890

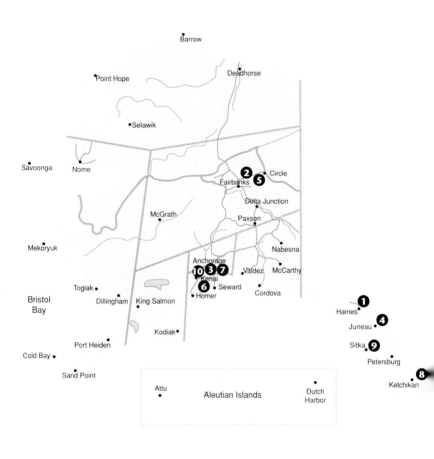

10 HIKES

❶ CHILKOOT TRAIL 33 mi.* (53 km)
Once used by Native Alaskans as a trading route to Canada, this popular
historic trail was travelled by thousands during the Klondike gold rush.
Terrain is difficult and elevation gain is 3,700 ft. (1,127 m). Allow 3-5 days.

❷ PINNELL MOUNTAIN NATIONAL RECREATION TRAIL 24 mi. (38.6 km)
Rugged trail near Fairbanks follows a series of alpine ridges above the treeline and offers spectacular views of the Alaska Range and the Yukon Flats.
The sun never sets on the trail in late June. Allow at least three days to complete the hike.

❸ TONY KNOWLES COASTAL TRAIL 11 mi. (17.7 km)
Paved trail stretching from downtown Anchorage to Kincaid Park is popular
with cyclists, joggers, skiers and birdwatchers. Trail offers scenic views of the
Cook Inlet, Mt. Susitna and Mt. McKinley.

❹ PERSEVERANCE TRAIL 3 mi. (4.8 km)
Popular trail system leading out of Juneau includes the Perseverance, Mt.
Juneau and Granite Creek trails. Highlight is view of the scenic Ebner Falls
that cascade more than 3,500 ft. (1,067 m) down Mt. Juneau.

❺ GRANITE TORS TRAIL 15 mi. loop (24 km)
Trail within the Chena Springs State Recreation Area leads to an unusual
grouping of volcanic spires that rise up to 200 ft. (61 m) above the surrounding tundra.

❻ HARDING ICEFIELD TRAIL 3.5 mi. (5.6 km)
Popular trail in Kenai Fjords National Park offers spectacular views of Exit
Glacier that descends 1/2 mile (.8 km) from Harding Icefield to the ocean
over 3 miles (4.8 km).

❼ JOHNSON ARM TRAIL 9.4 mi. (15.1 km)
Well-maintained trail in Chugach State Park parallels the coastline and provides scenic views of Turnagain Arm.

❽ PUNCHBOWL LAKE TRAIL .8 mi. (1.3 km)
Although this trail must be accessed by boat or plane, many believe it to be
the most scenic trail in the Misty Fjords National Monument and well worth
the trouble. Highlights include a waterfall and scenic Punchbowl Cove surrounded by vertical cliffs over 3,000 ft. (914 m) tall.

❾ INDIAN RIVER TRAIL 5.5 mi. (8.8 km)
Trail near downtown Sitka follows the Indian River through the coastal rainforest to scenic Indian River Falls.

❿ RESURRECTION PASS TRAIL SYSTEM 35 mi. (56 km)
Popular trail in Chugach National Forest renowned for its scenery and excellent lake fishing. Six public-use cabins on the trail can be booked in advance.

* All distances are for one-way trips unless otherwise indicated.

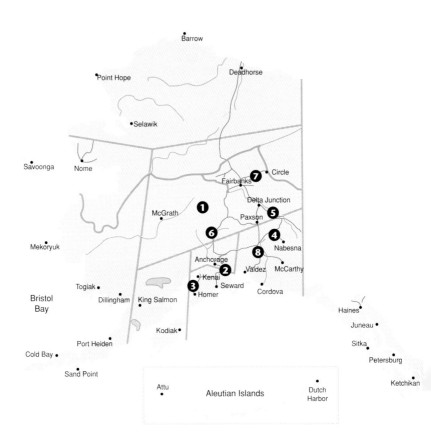

Barrow

Point Hope

Deadhorse

Selawik

Savoonga

Nome

Circle

7

Fairbanks

Delta Junction

McGrath

1

Paxson

5

Mekoryuk

6

4

Nabesna

Anchorage

8

McCarthy

Valdez

2

Kenai

Seward

Cordova

3

Homer

Togiak

Dillingham

King Salmon

Bristol
Bay

Haines

Juneau

Kodiak

Sitka

Port Heiden

Petersburg

Cold Bay

Ketchikan

Sand Point

Attu

Aleutian Islands

Dutch
Harbor

8 SCENIC DRIVES

Practically every drive through Alaska – even to the post office – is a scenic drive. The following lists a few of the better-known routes.

1 DENALI SHUTTLE 65 mi.* (105 km)
Shuttle bus ride into the heart of Denali National Park gives visitors the opportunity to see grizzlies, Dall sheep, wolves, caribou and the highest mountain in North America – Mt. McKinley – in a single day. Round-trip takes about 7.5 hours.

2 SEWARD HIGHWAY 127 mi. (204 km)
Connecting the cities of Anchorage and Seward, this drive highlights ice-blue glaciers, saltwater bays, lush valleys and native wildlife. Passes along the north shore of Turnagain Arm and offers panoramic views of the Kenai Mountains.

3 STERLING HIGHWAY 137 mi. (220 km)
Scenic highway winds through the Kenai Mountains to some of the best clamming beaches in the state and the picturesque hamlet of Homer. Lakes along the highway offer excellent fishing.

4 NABESNA ROAD 46 mi. (42 km)
Gravel road leading to the heart of Wrangell – St. Elias National Park winds through scenic wilderness encompassing a number of lakes.

5 ALASKA HIGHWAY 1,422 mi. (2,288 km)
Historic highway leading from Delta Junction to Dawson Creek, B.C. rolls through the wilderness. The 302 miles (486 km) of the highway found in Alaska traverse the eastern edge of the interior and along the Tanana River north of Tok.

6 GEORGE PARKS HIGHWAY 358 mi. (576 km)
This highway connecting Anchorage and Fairbanks passes through some of the most spectacular scenery in the state. Glaciers, dozens of rivers, and the awesome peaks of the Alaska Range are a few of the attractions along the route.

7 STEESE HIGHWAY 162 mi. (261 km)
Paved/gravel road is the oldest travel route through the interior. Branching highway connects Fairbanks with Circle Hot Springs, Chena Hot Springs and the town of Circle. Excellent wildflower viewing sites en route.

8 RICHARDSON HIGHWAY 368 mi. (592 km)
Scenic route from Valdez to Delta Junction winds through spruce forests and tundra meadows past several glaciers. Highlights the spectacular scenery of both the Chugach and Alaska Ranges.

* All distances are for one-way trips unless otherwise indicated.

When you travel into Alaska's wilderness, take the necessary precautions to ensure your dream trip doesn't end up a nightmare:

HIKING & CAMPING

1. Be self-sufficient when travelling. Don't expect to find fuel and/or food along the way. Wood is non-existent in many areas.

2. Remember that rugged terrain is subject to harsh weather that can change quickly. High winds, driving rain, sleet or snow can come about with little warning. Pack foul weather gear, food, matches and water whenever you head into the wilderness.

3. Be prepared to encounter wild animals and know how to react. Moose can be as dangerous as bears, especially cows with calves.

4. Biting flies and mosquitos can ruin the best of days. Your best defense is to dress in long pants and long-sleeved shirts and bring plenty of insect repellent. A head net is a good investment if travelling in late spring and early summer.

5. Filter or treat all drinking water to avoid giardia and other water-borne illnesses.

6. Carry a complete first aid kit and know how to deal with emergency situations. Be especially aware of the symptoms and treatment of hypothermia and exhaustion.

7. Keep campsites clean. Food and garbage must be stored in bear-proof containers that can be suspended in trees well away from camp.

8. Don't harrass wildlife to get better pictures. Spotting scopes and long lenses are essential to make the most of your wildlife viewing opportunities.

9. Keep pets at home or in your vehicle. They can potentially disturb and/or injure wild animals and may catch diseases.

BEAR AWARENESS

While it is relatively unlikely hikers will encounter bears in their back-country travels, it is possible. Read, *The Bears and You*, published by the Alaska Department of Fish & Game. Key points to remember are:

To avoid bears:

• Make noise when hiking, especially through brushy areas.

• If you smell carrion or garbage or see bear tracks or scat, leave the area.

• Bears are constantly looking for something to eat. Be sure to avoid contaminating your clothes and tents with food or food smells. Avoid using scented deodorants and soaps.

If you see a bear:

• Leave the area immediately, travelling downwind. **NEVER** get between a sow and her young.

If approached by a bear.

1) Identify yourself - Make yourself larger by waving your arms in the air. Talk in a normal voice and back away slowly. If it stands on its back legs, it is likely only curious. Avoid making direct eye contact as this can be perceived as a threat.

2) If it comes closer, stop backing away - Make loud noises by yelling and banging pots. **NEVER RUN** – you can't outrun a bear and doing so will stimulate it to attack.

3) If it charges - **DON'T RUN**. Shield yourself and ready your bear spray or other defenses. Bears will often make bluff charges without making contact to scare intruders away.

4) If it makes contact - Fall down and play dead - curl up in a ball with your hands behind your head. A bear will usually break off its attack if it feels the threat has been eliminated. Remain motionless and silent as long as possible. If a bear continues mauling, fight back aggressively. Try to punch it in the nose and gouge its eyes.

N.B. -   It is impossible to accurately predict bear behavior and the above is intended to provide general information only. The publisher assumes no responsibility for injuries sustained by individuals who follow these guidelines.

SPECIES CHECKLIST

CHECKLIST OF ALASKAN SPECIES FOUND IN THIS GUIDE

MAMMALS

❏ Masked Shrew
❏ Little Brown Bat
❏ Snowshoe Hare
❏ Collared Pika
❏ Red Squirrel
❏ Northern Flying Squirrel
❏ Hoary Marmot
❏ Arctic Ground Squirrel
❏ Beaver
❏ Deer Mouse
❏ Northern Red-backed Vole
❏ Muskrat
❏ Brown Lemming
❏ Porcupine
❏ Short-tailed Weasel
❏ Mink
❏ Marten
❏ Wolverine
❏ River Otter
❏ Sea Otter
❏ Arctic Fox
❏ Red Fox
❏ Gray Wolf
❏ Lynx
❏ Black Bear
❏ Brown Bear
❏ Sitka Black-tailed Deer
❏ Caribou
❏ Dall Sheep
❏ Moose
❏ Mountain Goat
❏ Muskox
❏ Polar Bear
❏ Pacific Walrus
❏ Northern Sea Lion
❏ Harbor Seal
❏ Pacific White-sided Dolphin
❏ Harbor Porpoise
❏ Dall's Porpoise
❏ Beluga Whale
❏ Humpback Whale
❏ Gray Whale
❏ Bowhead Whale
❏ Killer Whale

BIRDS

❏ Common Loon
❏ Red-throated Loon
❏ Red-necked Grebe
❏ Double-crested Cormorant
❏ Great Blue Heron
❏ Sandhill Crane
❏ Tundra Swan
❏ Canada Goose
❏ White-fronted Goose
❏ Emperor Goose
❏ Brant Goose
❏ Green-winged Teal
❏ Mallard
❏ Bufflehead
❏ Northern Pintail
❏ Northern Shoveler
❏ Greater Scaup
❏ Oldsquaw
❏ Harlequin Duck
❏ Common Goldeneye
❏ Common Eider
❏ King Eider
❏ White-winged Scoter
❏ Sharp-shinned Hawk
❏ Bald Eagle
❏ Red-tailed Hawk
❏ Golden Eagle
❏ Peregrine Falcon
❏ Spruce Grouse
❏ Ruffed Grouse
❏ Willow Ptarmigan
❏ Semi-palmated Plover
❏ Black-bellied Plover
❏ Spotted Sandpiper

❏ Least Sandpiper
❏ Western Sandpiper
❏ Dunlin
❏ Greater Yellowlegs
❏ Lesser Yellowlegs
❏ Red-necked Phalarope
❏ Black Oystercatcher
❏ Common Snipe
❏ Glaucous-winged Gull
❏ Herring Gull
❏ Bonaparte's Gull
❏ Black-legged Kittiwake
❏ Arctic Tern
❏ Long-tailed Jaeger
❏ Horned Puffin
❏ Pigeon Guillemot
❏ Marbled Murrelet
❏ Common Murre
❏ Rock Dove
❏ Great Horned Owl
❏ Short-eared Owl
❏ Snowy Owl
❏ Rufous Hummingbird
❏ Belted Kingfisher
❏ Downy Woodpecker
❏ Three-toed Woodpecker
❏ Northern Flicker
❏ Olive-sided Flycatcher
❏ Horned Lark
❏ Barn Swallow
❏ Tree Swallow
❏ Common Raven
❏ Steller's Jay
❏ Gray Jay
❏ Black-billed Magpie
❏ Red-breasted Nuthatch
❏ Black-capped Chickadee
❏ Boreal Chickadee
❏ American Dipper
❏ Golden-crowned Kinglet
❏ American Robin

❏ Varied Thrush
❏ Bohemian Waxwing
❏ Yellow Warbler
❏ Yellow-rumped Warbler
❏ Orange-crowned Warbler
❏ Common Redpoll
❏ Lapland Longspur
❏ Snow Bunting
❏ Savannah Sparrow
❏ Pine Grosbeak
❏ Dark-eyed Junco

AMPHIBIANS

❏ Wood Frog
❏ Boreal Toad

FISHES

❏ Pacific Lamprey
❏ Spiny Dogfish
❏ Pacific Herring
❏ Sheefish
❏ Rainbow Trout
❏ Lake Trout
❏ Arctic Char
❏ Dolly Varden
❏ Arctic Grayling
❏ Coho Salmon
❏ Sockeye Salmon
❏ Chum Salmon
❏ Pink Salmon
❏ Chinook Salmon
❏ Eulachon
❏ Alaska Blackfish
❏ Northern Pike
❏ Longnose Sucker
❏ Burbot

SPECIES CHECKLIST

❏ Walleye Pollock
❏ Ninespine Stickleback
❏ Yelloweye Rockfish
❏ Copper Rockfish
❏ Lingcod
❏ Kelp Greenling
❏ Slimy Sculpin
❏ Pacific Halibut

SEASHORE LIFE

❏ Bull Kelp
❏ Rockweed
❏ Eelgrass
❏ Surf Grass
❏ Sea Sack
❏ Sea Lettuce
❏ Giant Green Anemone
❏ Aggregate Anemone
❏ Brooding Anemone
❏ Frilled Anemone
❏ Moon Jellyfish
❏ Lion's Mane Jellyfish
❏ Ochre Sea Star
❏ Giant Spined Sea Star
❏ Daisy Brittle Star
❏ Bat Star
❏ Sand Dollar
❏ Purple Sea Urchin
❏ Green Sea Urchin
❏ Alaskan King Crab
❏ Dungeness Crab
❏ Purple Shore Crab
❏ Red Crab
❏ Hermit Crab
❏ Shrimp
❏ Acorn Barnacle
❏ Gooseneck Barnacle
❏ Rough Keyhole Limpet
❏ Lined Chiton
❏ Alaskan Abalone
❏ Native Littleneck Clam
❏ Pacific Razor Clam

❏ California Mussel
❏ Nuttall's Cockle
❏ Blue Mussel
❏ Pacific Weathervane Scallop
❏ Pacific Pink Scallop

TREES & SHRUBS

❏ Shore Pine
❏ Sitka Spruce
❏ Black Spruce
❏ White Spruce
❏ Western Hemlock
❏ Tamarack
❏ Alaska Cedar
❏ Common Juniper
❏ Bebb Willow
❏ Feltleaf Willow
❏ Quaking Aspen
❏ Balsam Poplar
❏ Paper Birch
❏ Sitka Alder
❏ Green Alder
❏ Douglas Maple
❏ Northern Red Currant
❏ Salmonberry
❏ Cloudberry
❏ Trailing Raspberry
❏ Soapberry
❏ Low Bush Cranberry
❏ High Bush Cranberry
❏ Kinnikinnik
❏ Bog Blueberry
❏ Pacific Serviceberry
❏ Crowberry
❏ Oregon Crab Apple
❏ Devil's Club
❏ Dwarf Arctic Birch
❏ Sweet Gale
❏ Red-Osier Dogwood

WILDFLOWERS

White

- ❏ Wild Calla
- ❏ Pussytoes
- ❏ Alaska Spirea
- ❏ Diapensia
- ❏ Single Delight
- ❏ Alp Lily
- ❏ Twisted Stalk
- ❏ Beach Strawberry
- ❏ Wild Celery
- ❏ Goatsbeard
- ❏ Three-leaved Foamflower
- ❏ Bunchberry
- ❏ Leatherleaf
- ❏ Labrador Tea
- ❏ Buckbean
- ❏ Moss Heather
- ❏ Death Camas
- ❏ Gold Thread
- ❏ Starflower
- ❏ Yarrow
- ❏ Narcissus Anemone
- ❏ Northern Bedstraw
- ❏ Cow Parsnip
- ❏ White Clover
- ❏ Arrow-leaved Coltsfoot
- ❏ Cotton Grass
- ❏ Mouse Ear Chickweed
- ❏ Grass of Parnassus

Yellow, Orange & Green

- ❏ Common Monkey Flower
- ❏ Yellow Dryas
- ❏ Woolly Mullein
- ❏ Yellow Pond Lily
- ❏ Toadflax
- ❏ Yellow Oxytrope
- ❏ Shrubby Cinequefoil
- ❏ Stream Violet

- ❏ Alaska Poppy
- ❏ Northern Green Bog Orchid
- ❏ Indian Hellebore
- ❏ Chocolate Lily
- ❏ Eschscholtz Buttercup
- ❏ Marsh Marigold
- ❏ Common Dandelion
- ❏ Common Plantain
- ❏ Horsetail

Red & Pink

- ❏ Bog Rosemary
- ❏ Fireweed
- ❏ Indian Paintbrush
- ❏ Red Columbine
- ❏ Roseroot
- ❏ Alpine Azalea
- ❏ Eskimo Potato
- ❏ Prickly Rose
- ❏ Shooting Star
- ❏ Twin Flower
- ❏ Arctic Dock
- ❏ Common Fleabane
- ❏ Round-leaved Sundew
- ❏ Ground Cone

Blue & Purple

- ❏ Alpine Forget-me-not
- ❏ Inky Gentian
- ❏ Arctic Lupine
- ❏ Monkshood
- ❏ Tall Larkspur
- ❏ Siberian Aster
- ❏ Harebell
- ❏ Arctic Lupine
- ❏ Purple Mountain Saxifrage
- ❏ Wild Iris
- ❏ Bluebells
- ❏ Wild Blue Flax

Alternate
Spaced singly along the stem.

Anther
The part of the stamen that produces pollen.

Albino
An animal lacking external pigmentation.

Anadromous
Organisms that live in saltwater and reproduce in freshwater.

Annual
A plant which completes its life cycle in one year.

Anterior
Pertaining to the front end.

Aquatic
Living in water.

Ascending
Rising or curving upward.

Barbel
An organ near the mouth of fish used to taste, touch, or smell.

Berry
A fruit formed of a single ovary which is fleshy or pulpy and contains one or many seeds.

Bloom
A whitish powdery or waxy covering.

Brackish
Water that is part freshwater and part saltwater.

Bract
A modified – often scale-like – leaf, usually small.

Branchlet
A twig from which leaves grow.

Boss
A rounded knob between the eyes of some toads.

Burrow
A tunnel excavated and inhabited by an animal.

Carnivorous
Feeding primarily on meat.

Catkin
A caterpillar-like drooping cluster of small flowers.

Cold-blooded
Refers to animals which are unable to regulate their own body temperature. 'Ectotherm' is the preferred term for this characteristic since many 'cold-blooded' species like reptiles are at times able to maintain a warmer body temperature than that of 'warm-blooded' species like mammals.

Conifer
A cone-bearing tree, usually evergreen.

Coverts
Small feathers that cover the top (uppertail) or underside (undertail) of the base of a bird's tail.

Deciduous
Shedding leaves annually.

Diurnal
Active primarily during the day.

Dorsal
Pertaining to the back or upper surface.

Ecology
The study of the relationships between organisms, and between organisms and their environment.

Flower
Reproductive structure of a plant.

Flower stalk
The stem bearing the flowers.

Fruit
The matured, seed-bearing ovary.

Habitat
The physical area in which organisms live.

Herbivorous
Feeding primarily on vegetation.

Insectivorous
Feeding primarily on insects.

Introduced
Species brought by humans to an area outside its normal range.

Invertebrate
Animals lacking backbones, e.g., worms, slugs, crustaceans, insects, shellfish.

Larva
Immature forms of an animal which differ from the adult.

Lateral
Located away from the mid-line, at or near the sides.

Lobe
A projecting part of a leaf or flower, usually rounded.

Molting
Loss of feathers, hair or skin while renewing plumage, coat or scales.

Morphs
A color variation of a species that is regular and not related to sex, age or season.

Nest
A structure built for shelter or insulation.

Nocturnal
Active primarily at night.

Omnivorous
Feeding on both animal and vegetable matter.

Ovary
The female sex organ which is the site of egg production and maturation.

Perennial
A plant that lives for several years.

Petal
The colored outer parts of a flower head.

Phase
Coloration other than normal.

Pistil
The central organ of the flower which develops into a fruit.

Pollen
The tiny grains produced in the anthers which contain the male reproductive cells.

Posterior
Pertaining to the rear.

Sepal
The outer, usually green, leaf-like structures that protect the flower bud and are located at the base of an open flower.

Species
A group of interbreeding organisms which are reproductively isolated from other groups.

Speculum
A brightly colored, iridescent patch on the wings of some birds, especially ducks.

Spur
A pointed projection.

Subspecies
A relatively uniform, distinct portion of a species population.

Ungulate
A hoofed mammal.

Ventral
Pertaining to the under or lower surface.

Vertebrate
An animal possessing a backbone.

Warm-blooded
An animal which regulates its blood temperature internally. 'Endotherm' is the preferred term for this characteristic.

Whorl
A circle of leaves or flowers about a stem.

Woolly
Bearing long or matted hairs.

BIBLIOGRAPHY

MAMMALS

Burt, W.H., and Grossenheider, R.P. *A Field Guide to the Mammals of America North of Mexico.* Houghton Mifflin, Boston, MA, 1976.

Halfpenny, J.C. *A Field Guide to Mammal Tracking in North America.* Johnson Books, Boulder, CO, 1986.

Hull, Cheryl et al. *Wildlife Notebook Series.* Alaska Department of Fish and Game, Juneau, AK, 1994.

Murie, O.J. *A Field Guide to Animal Tracks.* Houghton Mifflin, Boston, MA, 1975.

Rearden, J. *Mammals of Alaska.* Alaska Northwest Publishing Company, Anchorage, AK, 1981.

Smith, Dave. *Alaska's Mammals: A Guide to Selected Species.* Alaska Northwest Books, Seattle, WA, 1995.

Whitaker, J.D. *The Audubon Society Field Guide to North American Mammals.* A. Knopf, New York, NY, 1980.

BIRDS

Armstrong, R.H. *Guide to the Birds of Alaska.* Alaska Northwest Books, Seattle, WA, 1995.

Peterson, R.T. *A Field Guide to the Western Birds.* Houghton Mifflin, Boston, MA, 1990.

Robbins, C.S. et al. *Birds of North America.* Golden Press, New York, NY, 1988.

Udvardy, M.D.F. *The Audubon Society Field Guide to North American Birds – Western Region.* A. Knopf, New York, NY, 1977.

REPTILES & AMPHIBIANS

Behler, J.L., and King, F.W. *The Audubon Society Field Guide to North American Reptiles and Amphibians.* A. Knopf, New York, NY, 1979.

Hodge, J.P. *Reptiles and Amphibians in Alaska, the Yukon, and Northwest Territories.* Alaska Northwest Publishing Company, Anchorage, AK, 1976.

FISHES AND SEASHORE LIFE

Boschung, H.T. et al. *The Audubon Society Field Guide to North American Fishes, Whales and Dolphins.* Alfred Knopf, New York, NY, 1989.

Kessler, Doyne W. *Alaska's Saltwater Fishes and Other Sea Life.* Alaska Northwest Books, Seattle, WA, 1985.

McConnaughey, Bayard H. et al. *Pacific Coast.* Alfred A Knopf, New York, NY, 1985.

Morrow, J.E. *An Illustrated Key to the Freshwater Fishes of Alaska*. Alaska Northwest Books, Seattle, WA, 1980.

Page, L.M., and Burr, B.M. *A Field Guide to Freshwater Fishes*. Houghton Mifflin, Boston, MA, 1991.

Rehder, H.A. *The Audubon Society Guide to North American Seashells*. Alfred Knopf, New York, NY, 1981.

FLORA

Brockman, C.F. *Trees of North America*. Golden Press, New York, NY, 1979.

Clark, Lewis J. *Wildflowers of the Pacific Northwest*. Gray's Publishing, Sidney, BC, 1976.

Little, E.L. *The Audubon Society Field Guide to North American Trees – Western Region*. A. Knopf, New York, NY, 1979.

Heller, Christine. *Wild, Edible and Poisonous Plants of Alaska*. Alaska Natural History Association, Anchorage, AK, 1990.

Hulten, E. *Flora of Alaska and Neighboring Territories*. Stanford University Press, Stanford, CA, 1968.

Pratt, Verna. *Alaskan Wildflowers*. Alaskakrafts, Anchorage, AK, 1989.

Spellenberg, R. *The Audubon Society Field Guide to North American Wildflowers – Western Region*. A. Knopf, New York, NY, 1979.

Venning, D. *Wildflowers of North America*. Golden Press, New York, NY, 1984.

Viereck, Leslie A. and Little, Elbert J. Jr. *Alaska Trees and Shrubs*. University of Alaska Press, Fairbanks, AK, 1988.

Welsh, Stanley L. *Anderson's Flora of Alaska*. Brigham Young University Press, Provo, UT, 1974.

NATURAL HISTORY

Ewing, Susan. *The Great Alaska Nature Factbook*. Alaska Northwest Books, Anchorage, AK, 1996.

Hedin, Robert et al. *Alaska: Reflections on Land and Spirit*. University of Arizona Press, Tucson, AZ, 1989.

O'Clair, Rita M., Armstrong, Robert H. and Carstensen, Richard. *The Nature of Southeast Alaska*. Alaska Northwest Books, Seattle, WA, 1992.

Stonehouse, Bernard *Animals of the Arctic: The Ecology of the Far North*. Holt, Reinhart & Winston, New York, NY, 1971.

RESOURCES

Alaska Department of Fish and Game
333 Raspberry Road, Anchorage, AK 99518 (907) 267-2351
or
PO Box 25526, Juneau, AK 99802 (907) 465-4100

Alaska Division of Parks and Outdoor Recreation
3601 C Street, Anchorage, AK 99503-5921 (907) 269-8700

Alaska Natural History Association
605 West 4th Avenue, Suite 85, Anchorage, AK 99501 (907) 274-8440

Alaska Public Lands Information Center
605 West 4th Avenue, Suite 105, Anchorage, AK 99501 (907) 271-2737

Alaska State Bureau of Land Management
222 West 7th Ave., Suite 13, Anchorage, AK 99513 (907) 271-5960

Alaska Tourism Office
PO Box 110801, Juneau, AK 99811 (907) 465-2010

Alaska Native Tourism Council
1577 C Street, Suite 304, Anchorage, AK 99501 (907) 274-5400

Alaska Ferry System
PO Box 25535-5535, Juneau, AK 99802 (800) 642-0066

Audubon Society – Alaska Regional Office
308 G Street, Suite 217, Anchorage, AK 99501 (907) 276-7034

Discovery Foundation (non-profit outdoor educational organization)
PO Box 21867, Juneau, AK 99802 (907) 463-1500

US Forest Service – Alaska Regional Office
PO Box 21628, Juneau, AK 99802 (907) 586-8863

US Fish and Wildlife Service – Alaska Regional Office
1011 East Tudor Road, Anchorage, AK 99503 (907) 786-3486

INDEX

FROM WATERFORD PRESS

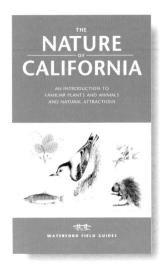
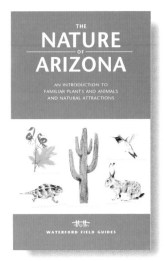
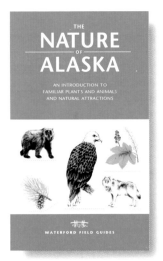
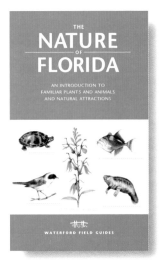